Growing Past Kant

By Jim Trader

Fifth Estate

2795 County Hwy 57

Blountsville, AL 35031

First Edition

Cover Designed by An Quigley

Printed on acid-free paper

Library of Congress Control No: 2011945829
ISBN: 9781936533213

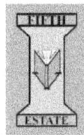

Fifth Estate, 2011

Table of Contents

Blessed am I, for it is granted unto me to know the multiplicity and diversity of the gods. Woe unto you, for you have substituted the oneness of God for the diversity which cannot be resolved into the one. Through this you have created the torment of incomprehension, and the mutilation of the created world, the essence and law of which is diversity. How can you be true to your nature when you attempt to make one out of the many? What you do to the gods, that also befalls you. All of you are made thus the same and in this way your nature also becomes mutilated.

-Carl Jung, "The Seven Sermons To The Dead"

Introduction

Something went wrong with the 20th Century. While tremendous advances were made in the fields of nuclear physics, psychology, and economics, many of the issues these studies are supposed to address—harmful natural forces, individual maladjustment, and economic inequality—seem even more of a problem in 2011 than they were in 1911. With seemingly uncontrollable environmental deterioration (acid rain, respiratory problems resulting from pollution, an increasing lack of drinkable water), a looming energy crisis, a world-wide widening of the economic gap between rich and poor, and increasing personal depression and social apathy in the U.S., one wonders how much good was really done by the observations of Einstein, the psychoanalysis of Freud, or the economic theories of John Maynard Keynes. It's possible that if we don't find an answer to what went wrong with the 20th Century, the quality of our individual and collective lives will continue to deteriorate during the 21st.

When searching for these answers, it may be profitable to look into one field of study that has not appreciably advanced since the 19th Century: Philosophy. While it may seem farfetched when stated baldly, it becomes evident on close study that many of the advances— and limitations—of modern thought have as their foundation the supremacy of intellect, the reductionism, and the interplay of opposites that culminated in 19th Century philosophy.

It also becomes evident, through observation, that a culture based primarily on these principles is not sustainable. The knowledge we have acquired through exclusive use of the tools of 19th Century philosophy, though profitable in the short-term, has begun to outlive its usefulness here at the beginning of the 21st Century. While these tools have been undeniably useful in shaping the world we have now, more and different tools are required if we are to shape a sustainable world.

Obviously, we need these new tools. And that is part of what this book is here to provide. After a careful analysis of how pre-20th Century philosophy has been the tool used to fashion the thinking and the science of the 20th Century—both its benefits and its shortcomings—this book describes and considers a potential new tool and some of the uses to which it may be put.

Much of the 20th Century has been wonderful, and what damage has been done is still reversible. It is not the purpose of this book to eliminate our hard-won intellectual tools or the technology that has sprung from them; merely to point out that, if one is going to build a house, one needs more than just a saw and wood.

What Happened?

Rome wasn't built in a day, and neither was the edifice of modern thought. This chapter will trace the development of our modern intellectual "toolbox," so we can see what we did right, and where we may still have some things to learn. This is by no means a comprehensive overview of the philosophies discussed (those of Descartes, Kant, Hegel, and Nietzsche), merely a summary of the contributions from each that can be traced to them from outside the field of philosophy, and the contributions of each that successive philosophers built upon.

Doubting Descartes

For the full picture of 19th Century philosophy and how it applies to the modern world, one must start in France, in the year 1644, with the publication of Rene' Descartes' "Principles of Philosophy." While his expression *cogito ergo sum* (I think, therefore I am) has become quite famous as the herald-cry of modern thought, it is worth quoting in context here:

"VII. That we cannot doubt of our existence while we doubt, and that this is the first knowledge we acquire when we philosophize in order.

While we thus reject all of which we can entertain the smallest doubt, and even imagine that it is false, we easily indeed suppose there is neither a God, nor sky, nor bodies, nor hands, nor feet, nor, finally, a body; but we cannot in the same way suppose that we are not while we doubt of the truth of things; for there is a repugnance in conceiving that what thinks does not exist at the very time when it thinks. Accordingly, this knowledge, *I think, therefore I am*, is the first and most certain that occurs to one who philosophises orderly." (italics in original)[1]

Not only is Descartes advising his readers to doubt, but he is stating that the ability to doubt—and by extension, the ability to think—is the prerequisite of conscious existence. By first determining that oneself actually exists—through being able to think/doubt, and therefore verify one's existence "beyond doubt"—one is then able to examine (think about/doubt) the rest of the universe, and determine what is "real" or "true" (a thing is real/true if it is beyond doubt). This primacy of mind, its proof of primacy through deconstruction—doubt—of all perceived phenomena to their basic, or "real," principles, and the ability to acquire new knowledge through the application of these "real" principles, is the process which is Descartes' legacy to us all.[2]

Descartes' system of thought was quite revolutionary in his time; not only were all European scholastic institutions dominated by the Roman Catholic Church (an organization not known for its tolerance of doubt), but much of the curriculum was simple rote, based on the authorities of Aristotle, Ptolemy, and Galen, and accepted as true without ever being questioned or tested[3]. By creating a method of understanding—a "philosophy"—that took nothing for granted, and that could be used by anyone to understand anything, Descartes opened a door to the expansion of understanding that has made our modern miracles possible. Descartes did us all a huge favor, by pioneering the idea of independent intellectual inquiry, and by demonstrating through its success the limitations of "received truth" (knowledge accepted as true without examination).

Descartes' philosophy, however, was not without its own limitations. Having designed his philosophy primarily as a means to study the physical world, it turned out to have limited application to the physical world; Descartes used his philosophical system to plumb the depths of physics, psychology, mathematics, ethics, logic, and medicine, yet none of his contributions in these areas have withstood the test of time except in mathematics.[4]

Nevertheless, Descartes also set another important precedent by his scientific explorations, which future philosophers were to follow: As well as systemizing a way for the mind to acquire and process knowledge, this system is in a form that reflects (or attempts to reflect) the physical sciences and mathematics[5], and uses the sciences and mathematics as benchmarks to demonstrate its (philosophy's) effectiveness. While later philosophers and scientists were to disagree with the results of Descartes' work, the process by which he arrived at his results has continued to be used by

contributors to both the hard and soft sciences. This phenomenon—
the criticizing of results while accepting and even praising the process
that produced the results—appears to be a keynote of modern
philosophy and modern thought, and is one of the essential issues
examined in this work.

Kant's Contradiction

It has been said that all modern philosophy after Kant, is
merely a set of footnotes to Kant's work. If Descartes would be
considered the John the Baptist of modern philosophy, crying out in
the academic wilderness of his time a revolutionary message of
overturning the old Aristotelian order to make way for a coming Age
of Reason, many would consider Kant to be equivalent to Jesus.
Kant's Gospel—contained in the "Critique of Pure Reason"—has
indeed defined the scope and priorities of much of modern philosophy
since its publication in 1787, providing the rulebook, so to speak, of
philosophical discourse in the 19th and much of the 20th Centuries[6]. In
the spirit of Descartes, it may be time to examine the principles
(Kant's rules) by which philosophy has been operating, and see if
they are, indeed, "true" principles.

In Kant's system, different kinds of knowledge are very
precisely defined. There is *a priori* knowledge (also called "pure"
knowledge, which is knowledge independent of direct experience)
and *a posteriori* knowledge (also called "empirical" knowledge,
which is knowledge gained by direct experience).[7] According to Kant,
correct *a priori* knowledge is more useful—and therefore more
important—than correct *a posteriori* knowledge[8], and it was therefore
his intention to develop "a science which shall determine the
possibility, the principles, and the extent of all *a priori* knowledge".[9]
Knowledge of either kind is acquired through judgments, of which
there are two kinds: *synthetic* and *analytic.*[10] Of the two, *synthetic*
judgments (where the predicate is based on the subject) are the more
useful, since they add to knowledge, while *analytic* judgments (where

the predicate is contained in the subject) never do more than state what is already apparent, and so do not add to knowledge.[11] The statement "Jane likes skateboarding" (an example of a *synthetic* judgment) is usually considered more informative than "Jane is the name of a girl" (an example of an *analytic* judgment).

Another important division in Kantian thought is that between the logical *analytic* ("a logic of truth"[12]) and the logical *dialectic* ("a logic of illusion"[13]). This division between the *analytic* and *dialectic* is important because, according to Kant, only the logic of the *analytic* is useful for acquiring correct *a priori* knowledge; the logic of the *dialectic* produces only false assumptions (illusion).[14] And therein lies the contradiction—the paradox—of Kant's science of pure reason.

In his Preface to the Second Edition of the Critique, page xxi, Kant penned the following footnote:

"This experiment of pure reason bears a great similarity to what in chemistry is sometimes entitled the experiment of *reduction*, or more usually the *synthetic* process. The *analysis of the metaphysician* separates pure *a priori* knowledge into two very heterogeneous elements, namely, the knowledge of things as appearances, and the knowledge of things in themselves; his *dialectic* combines these two again, in *harmony* with the necessary idea of the *unconditioned* demanded by reason, and finds that this harmony can never be obtained except through the above distinction, which must therefore be accepted." (italics in original)

'This experiment of pure reason' to which Kant refers, is his experiment to prove—*a priori*—that the experience of all objects must conform to the concepts of those objects as appearances (and thereby demonstrate the usefulness of *a priori* knowledge in general)[15], which he concludes to his satisfaction. Essentially, Kant is telling us here that *accurate synthetic a priori judgments are impossible without the use of the dialectic*. Since the goal of Pure Reason, as Kant defines it, is to obtain accurate synthetic *a priori* judgments (as discussed above), and since Kant himself demonstrates that accurate synthetic *a priori* judgments are not obtainable without the use of the *dialectic*, his many statements of—and chapters on— the fact that the *dialectic* is the "logic of illusion" seem to undermine his whole philosophy. Since much of the Critique of Pure Reason is dedicated to proving the illusory nature of what he calls the Transcendental Dialectic[16], while at the same time his method of finding truth is dependent upon the use of the *dialectic*, we find ourselves back where we were before Kant penned his masterpiece: Unable to distinguish correct *a priori* judgments from incorrect ones except by observation, a method which Descartes already proved—through his mistakes—as unreliable at best.

So in our critique of Kant's Critique, it seems certain that the principles delineated—Kant's "science of metaphysics"[17]—cannot be considered "true" in Cartesian (or even Kantian) terms, based as they are on self-contradiction. Yet even with this fundamental contradiction revealed, Kant's contribution to modern thought cannot be denied. These principles, though "doubtable," apparently hold at least a grain of truth. It becomes obvious, especially after re-reading Kant's footnote quoted above, that the idea that has become known as the Hegelian dialectic (the interplay and ultimate synthesis of opposites through dialectic) was originally contained—ignored, maligned, but quite essential—in Kant's philosophic opus. This idea of the Hegelian dialectic, it will be shown in later chapters, has come to underlie all of 20th Century thought. Also, Kant—more so than Descartes—can be said to be the first to explicitly define philosophy as a science of *reduction*; not only does Kant describe the process of reduction as essential to his science of pure reason (see Kant's footnote quoted above), Kant states early on in his Critique that logic can never serve as more than a "negative touchstone of truth," identifying the form "pure" knowledge must take, yet remaining forever indifferent to the empirical content of that knowledge[18]; in other words, his system of "Pure Reason" was simply the reduction of all perceptions and experiences to their most basic principles. Kant thereby gave himself—and all philosophers to come after him—a way to avoid Descartes' error of inaccurate observations of the empirical world (the world of the senses), by simply saying that his business is only the reduction of perception to basic principles and the study of the interaction of these principles with each other, thereby relieving himself (and his successors) of the responsibility of making accurate empirical observations. Philosophy, as we typically understand the term today, was born.

These three basic concepts—the reduction of all things to a set of opposites, reality as the interplay of opposites, and the synthesis of opposites through dialectic—have come to underpin not only modern philosophy, but by the end of the 20th Century, all forms of thought and inquiry.

Kant certainly followed in Descartes' footsteps in proposing the supremacy of mind, as shown throughout his Critique by the supremacy of the *a priori* over the *a posteriori*. Also like Descartes, Kant based his system of thought on the physical sciences and mathematics[19], and he gave priority to the ability to derive new knowledge from established principles (albeit strictly *a priori* knowledge in Kant's system). Kant's main innovation to Descartes' method—other than defining "metaphysics" itself as a science, thereby creating what we know today as the study of "philosophy"— was in defining all phenomena as fundamentally dualistic (all phenomena can be reduced to exactly two opposing elements).

The stage had been set by Descartes, the sacred doctrine expounded by Kant. The full interpretation of the doctrine, however, had to wait for Hegel.

Hegel's Opposition

To carry the Biblical metaphor established in the previous section to its conclusion, if Descartes is the John the Baptist of modern thought, and Kant its Jesus, Hegel can be equated to St. Paul.

Hegel, while being quite vocal on the limitations of Kantian constructions[20], had no qualms about using Kant's essential process of reduction and synthesis of opposites through use of the dialectic as the basis of his (Hegel's) own philosophical system. In Hegel's opus "Science of Logic" (originally published in 1812), generally considered to contain the basis of his (Hegel's) entire philosophy, the very first chapter is devoted to outlining the Kantian synthetic process in the broadest of terms (reality is created by the synthesis of opposites, the *becoming* of *being* and *nothing*)[21], of which the rest of the book is a restatement of this process by its application to more narrowly defined terms (quantity, quality, measure, essence, ground, etc.)[22]. Hegel took the Kantian synthetic process one step further, however, by stating (and repeatedly "proving") that opposites are not only equal, but equivalent; in Hegel's logic there is *no difference* between *being* and *nothing* (or any of the other sets of opposites Hegel outlines in his book), we only experience a difference between them because we perceive their different stages of *becoming*. Also, Hegel proposed that while his Science of Logic (and the field of philosophy in general) overlaps some areas of mathematics, the Science of Logic is actually *superior* to mathematics in producing understanding[23]. It is these concepts—the equivalence of opposites, and the transcendence in Hegel's philosophy of Kant's and Descartes' adherence to mathematics—that truly set Hegel's philosophy apart from Kant's, and truly defines Hegel's unique contribution to modern thought. Everything else in his science of logic—the primacy of mind, the reduction of all phenomena to an essential duality, the testing of these dualistic elements for consistency, the use of the dialectic (i.e. *becoming*) to bring about synthesis—can all be traced back to Descartes, to Kant, or to both. Hegel just used different—and usually many more—words to state his position than his predecessors did, yet for all of these concepts (especially synthesis through use of the dialectic) it is Hegel who is generally thought of as their originator and champion. This is in some ways comparable to St. Paul's championing the Good News of Jesus, where Jesus' message—along with a couple of innovations original to Paul—was disseminated to the world, but while Jesus' message was retained in name and in principle, it was Paul's interpretation that was retained in fact.

A later chapter will address the usefulness—and limits—of the Cartesian-Kantian-Hegelian process (or C-K-H process) inside and outside the field of philosophy, but it will be instructive, first, to look at one other major philosopher since Hegel. It is the last piece of the puzzle in understanding the how and the why of modern philosophy's failure to advance.

Nietzsche's Reaction

Nietzsche, writing as he did toward the end of the 19th Century, can superficially be seen as reacting—and so providing a counterforce—to the rigid, airless rationalism of Hegel and Kant. It is revealed on deeper examination, however, that Nietzsche's philosophy was no such counterforce. Like Kant and Hegel before him, while Nietzsche disagreed with the results obtained by earlier philosophers, he believed their basic premises (and the process by which they were applied) were valid. Nietzsche did, however, make an original and powerful contribution to modern philosophy: he was the first to subtract from the modern philosophical process, rather than add, setting a precedent that philosophers are still following in the early 21st Century.

When first reading Nietzsche (especially his most popular work, "Thus Spake Zarathustra"), it is hard to see any connection between him and the ultra-rationalists that preceded him. The complete lack of logical argument, the reliance upon experience (and even unsupported *personal opinion*) to make his points, and his ubiquitous—and sometimes obscure—use of metaphor, all seem to indicate a renunciation of the carefully-kept philosophical estate that was his inheritance from Descartes, Kant and Hegel.

However, Nietzsche's thought is still discernable as a superstructure of the basic assumptions that Descartes outlined in his philosophy; it appears much like an inevitable but undesired and disheveled garage, attached to an otherwise immaculately maintained and organized house. Descartes' main legacy to modern philosophy— the primacy of mind, the proof of primacy through doubt, and the ability to find new knowledge through the application of "real" (beyond doubt) principles—is very apparent in Nietzsche's work, if one pays attention. Firstly, when Nietzsche pays homage to the importance of creativity as expressed through the spirit[24], his concept of "will"—the force of the spirit that creates—always seems to create primarily through thought (an idea or value), and only secondarily through action, thus indicating mind's primacy of place. Secondly, one of Nietzsche's philosophy's most celebrated traits is its irreverence for all intellectual and social institutions (especially religion and its attendant morality)[25]; this seems to be merely a continuation of Descartes' battle for the independence of people's minds in the 17th Century, where he encouraged people to doubt what they had been taught by rote (mostly through religious institutions and the schools these institutions controlled), and find their own verifiable truth through rational observation. Nietzsche simply extended this

19

"doubt" to moral as well as scholastic authority. Thirdly, Nietzsche has no hesitation to apply what he considers to be "true principles" (things beyond doubt) to the external world; the main differences here between Nietzsche and his predecessors, are that Nietzsche spends little time "proving" the truth of his first principles, and most of his time on general statements of his (as Kant might call them) synthetic judgments. Unfortunately, most of Nietzsche's synthetic judgments, such as the "will to power" and "the overman," never leave the realm of metaphor and generality, limiting the usefulness of his philosophical system. Nietzsche's philosophy makes sense if one already perceives the world as Nietzsche did, but there is little in his philosophy to convince a "camel" or a "lion" to "overcome" and become a "child".[26]

Moreover, Nietzsche was outspoken in his reverence for the C-K-H process of reduction-and-synthesis, even as he disparaged Kant's thrust of research and results. The following passage is illustrative of the point:

"Chemistry of concepts and feelings. In almost all respects, philosophical problems today are again formulated as they were two thousand years ago; how can something arise from its opposite—for example, reason from unreason, sensation from the lifeless, logic from the illogical, disinterested observation from covetous desire, altruism from ego, truth from error? Until now, metaphysical philosophy has overcome this difficulty by denying the origin of the one from the other, and by assuming for the more highly valued things some miraculous origin, directly from out of the heart and essence of the "thing in itself" [a reference to Kant's CoPR]. Historical philosophy, on the other hand, the very youngest of all philosophical methods, which can no longer be even considered as separate from the natural sciences, has determined in isolated cases (and will probably conclude in all of them) that they are not opposites, only exaggerated to be so by the popular or metaphysical view, and that this opposition is based on an error of reason. As historical philosophy explains it, there exists, strictly considered, neither a selfless act nor a completely disinterested observation: both are merely sublimations. In them the basic element appears to be virtually dispersed and proves to be present only to the most careful observer.

All we need, something which can be given us only now, with the various sciences at their present level of achievement, is a *chemistry* of moral, religious, ascetic ideas and feelings, a chemistry of those impulses that we ourselves experience in the great and small interactions of culture and society, indeed even in solitude. What if this chemistry might end with the conclusion that, even here, the most glorious colors are extracted from base, even despised substances? Are there many who will want to pursue such investigations? Mankind loves to put the questions of origin and beginnings out of mind: must one be almost inhuman to feel in himself the opposite inclination?" (italics in original)[27]

  This passage, the very first in Nietzsche's book "Human, All Too Human" Vol. 1 (the book where Nietzsche first came into his own as a philosopher), is very telling. Not only is Nietzsche disparaging his predecessor Kant's conclusions while at the same time extolling the need for a "chemistry of concepts and feelings"—as shown in an earlier section, the very metaphor Kant uses to describe how he arrives at his proofs—but he lauds the "Historical philosophy…which can no longer even be considered as separate from the natural sciences….", which is directly attributable to Hegel (Hegel's lectures that were to become the book "Philosophy of History" were originally delivered in 1830-31, while "Human, All Too Human" Vol. 1 was written between 1876 and 1878) and enshrines both Kant's and Hegel's goal of making philosophy—metaphysics—into a "science"[28].

  Nietzsche's innovation to the C-K-H process was to use only a part of the process, specifically *reduction*, to produce understanding. His major contribution to 20th Century thought appears to be his tendency to deconstruct (*reduce* to their basic elements) belief- and thought-systems, without thereafter rebuilding a useable structure from (a demonstrable "synthesis" of) the "true" principles so discovered; a precedent actually set by Kant in defining the process of understanding as one of reduction, which Nietzsche simply seized and expanded upon. The results of this innovation will be analyzed at some length in the discussion of Postmodernism, in the next Chapter.

What's Happening?

Just as the philosophies of Descartes, Kant and Hegel were fundamentally shaped by the science of their time, so was science in the 20th Century shaped by the philosophies of Descartes, Kant and Hegel. As much as philosophy is often dismissed in the early 21st Century as a waste of time, it is evident upon closer study that the philosophy of a century ago shapes the science, the study, and even the common perceptions of today.

In this chapter, three areas of science outside of philosophy that enjoyed major breakthroughs in the 20th Century—physics, psychology and economics—will be shown to have been indelibly shaped by the philosophical process laid out by Descartes, Kant and Hegel. Also in this chapter, the most recent genus of philosophy—post-modernism—will be discussed, as well as how post-modernism (like the philosophies before it) may presage what is to come in Western society and science.

Just as in the last chapter, where only those fundamentals of each philosopher's work that shaped 20th Century thought were discussed, so in this chapter only those corresponding fundamentals of each 20th Century field of study that most directly illustrate philosophy's influence will be examined.

It should also be noted, that the claim is not being made that any of the thinkers whose theories will be discussed in this chapter were conscious of the C-K-H process or its influence. While it is impossible to know one way or another, this work is proceeding based on the opposite assumption, that these various thinkers were *not* conscious of the C-K-H process' influence evident in their work, and therefore the theories discussed will be used as illustrations of how ubiquitous and taken for granted the C-K-H process became in 20th Century thought.

To demonstrate the pervasive influence of the Cartesian-Kantian-Hegelian process on 20th Century thought, it may be instructive to begin with a well-known theory that originated in 19th Century science, which is still in frequent use today. Like Nietzsche, while this example at first seems to leave the orbit of the C-K-H structure's solar system, it really only follows a comet-like course out of the philosophical plane of the ecliptic, its motions still predictable by the laws of Kantian gravity. This will throw into stark relief the more conventional examples that follow, whose underpinnings can be traced more easily to the C-K-H process.

Darwin's Deviation

In his classic "The Origin of Species," published in 1859, Darwin laid out in great detail what is now widely known as the theory of evolution. In brief, this theory states that living organisms were not originally as they are seen today, but rather began long ago in a single genus, which then developed variations on itself (mutated) to successfully adapt to different environments; thus different genera developed from the original, and each genus in turn specialized into species and then sub-species, each filling a separate niche in the local environment and ecology. Most importantly, this process is ongoing.

This process of continual adaptation and variation through mutation, now known as "evolution," has provided plausible explanations for certain otherwise-hard-to-explain phenomena (such as the fossil record and mutation), and is a cornerstone of modern-day biology[1]. At first glance, this theory has nothing to do with the principles or process of the C-K-H thought structure as previously described, and—since the theory of evolution could arguably be considered an underpinning of 20th Century thought, at least in biology—would therefore seem to weaken the case for the C-K-H process as underlying 20th Century thought and science. There is, however, more to this particular story.

In Kant's work "Critique of Pure Reason," in the chapter entitled "Regulative Employment of the Ideas Of Pure Reason," Kant discusses certain ideas that seem to him inherent to any application of reason. On pp536-45, Kant lays out a series of principles regarding the systemization of ideas that exactly corresponds to Darwin's theory of evolution, down to using the terminology "genus," "species" and "subspecies" to describe different levels of specificity of ideas. While this whole systemization would be ponderous to quote in full, a part of Kant's own commentary about these inherent traits of systemization bears repeating here:

"The remarkable feature of these principles, and what in them alone concerns us, is that they seem to be transcendental, and that although they contain mere ideas for the guidance of the empirical employment of reason—ideas which reason only follows as it were asymptotically, i.e. ever more closely without ever reaching them— they yet possess, as synthetic *a priori* propositions, objective but indeterminate validity, and serve as rules for possible experience. They can also be employed with great advantage in the elaboration of experience, as heuristic principles. A transcendental deduction of them cannot, however, be effected; in the case of ideas…such a deduction is never possible."[2]

Essentially, what Kant is saying is that while this systemization may have use as a set of guidelines for possible experience, it can never be conclusively proved as a set of guidelines for all experience. Although Kant was discussing a systemization of ideas, his commentary is apropos to Darwin's theory of evolution: While the theory has been very useful in explaining certain phenomena (fossil record, mutation), it is not perfect (origin of human beings, bananas, and a few others unexplained) and has never been proven; humanity has never seen "evolution in action" where there wasn't human intervention. While genetic manipulation (not to mention cross-breeding and cross-fertilization which, as Darwin pointed out, has been practiced since humans began farming and domesticating animals) may well re-create the stated effects of evolution, there is still no direct proof that this occurs in nature; only, in many cases, a high probability. We can never deduce, in the case of Darwin's theory, whether or not it is the whole story. As Kant said, "such a deduction is never possible." At the end of the 18th Century, Kant had already discovered and explicated what later became known as the theory of evolution, and shown it to be as much of a myth (i.e. an un-provable, only partially consistent, yet intuitively appealing hypothesis) as the theory of creationism. While the theory of evolution seems to explain more phenomena than the theory of creationism, and evolution has much greater appeal to the rational mind, both theories are—and will probably remain—essentially equal, in that they are both perspectives without the possibility of final vindication over each other.

Although most of the objections to the theory of evolution in the West are raised by the monotheistic religious community—who lose influence when the myth of evolution is accepted in place of the myth of creationism, and so have a vested interest in seeing it debunked—Kant's analysis handily explains why the case for evolution is never airtight, despite the evident applicability of Darwin's theory to a physical science and its "common sense" appeal.

It has been shown here how a basic tenet of modern science was thoroughly presaged and defined by modern philosophy, specifically that of Kant. The proceeding sections will illustrate in detail how modern thought was and is comprehensively shaped by the C-K-H process.

Synthesizing Physics

It would be hard to dispute the claim that Einstein's Theory of Relativity is the most significant contribution to physics made in the 20th Century. His Theory of Relativity has formed one of the two pillars of modern, or post-Newtonian, physics (the other pillar being quantum mechanics), and of the two pillars Einstein's theory has arguably added the most to our understanding, providing such breakthroughs as a more accurate theory of gravity, discovering the constancy of the speed of light, and the possibility of nuclear fission/fusion.

Before we discuss the theory's debt to the C-K-H process, a brief introduction to the theory itself is in order.

Einstein, in the Table of Contents of his book "Relativity," divided his Theory of Relativity into two parts, the Special (or Restricted) Theory of Relativity, and the General Theory of Relativity. His Special Theory, as he defines it, reads as:

"If, relative to K, K' is a uniformly moving co-ordinate system devoid of rotation, then natural phenomena run their course in respect to K' according to exactly the same general laws as with respect to K"[3]

The examples Einstein uses for "K" and "K'" are a railroad embankment (for K), and a train (for K'). So, while a train (K') moves relative to the embankment its tracks rest upon (K), observations made from either the train or the embankment of a phenomenon (Einstein used the example of a bird passing overhead) are equally valid descriptions of the phenomenon no matter how different those descriptions may be. According to the Special Theory, this is always true as long as the relative motions of the "co-ordinate systems" (train and tracks, in this case) "are in a state of *uniform rectilinear and non-rotatory motion* [italics in original]"[4]. This means that their motion relative to each other must be constant, proceed in a straight line, and not change direction.

Einstein described his General Theory of Relativity as:

"All bodies of reference K, K', etc. are equivalent for the description of natural phenomena (formulation of the general laws of nature), whatever may be their state of motion."[5]

The General Theory goes a step further than the Special Theory does, in saying that natural laws (and their observation) hold true no matter how two or more different co-ordinate systems are moving relative to each other. According to the General Theory of Relativity, the descriptions of any motion observable from the moving train (K'), its embankment (K), and, say, a helicopter flying overhead and banking away as part of a turn, are all equally valid, equally "real," despite the fact that they will all be quite different descriptions of the same phenomenon observed at the same time; a state of affairs impossible according to Newtonian physics. Such differences are negligible in the everyday world we live in, since we are not large enough or move fast enough for these differences to be significant. However, the differences are there—and thanks to improved instrumentation, are now measurable—and Einstein's theory has helped science predict and possibly understand the universe's behavior on a planetary-and-larger scale.

When most people think of Einstein and his Theory of Relativity, the first thing that comes to mind is the equation "$E=mc^2$". This equation, explained by Einstein in his book "Relativity" in the chapter "General Results of the Theory," combined two laws from Newtonian physics—the Law of Conservation of Mass and the Law of Conservation of Energy—into a single law which stated that a body's inertial mass is equivalent to the energy contained in that body[6] "provided that the system neither takes up nor sends out energy"[7]. Another way of stating this law is that as long as a body is not consuming or releasing energy, the amount of energy necessary to move the body is the same amount of energy contained in the body. As an example, if it takes five pounds of pressure to move a glass of water (whether it was at rest on a table, or already in motion towards one's mouth), that glass of water must exert five pounds of force on any other body it encounters (the table, one's hand, one's mouth). It was this equation that first opened physicists' eyes to the possibility of nuclear fission (the splitting apart of a heavy atom's nucleus, used in nuclear reactors and "atomic bombs") and nuclear fusion (a nuclear reaction in which two atomic nuclei merge to form a single, heavier nucleus, releasing energy in the process, how stars are thought to produce their energy and light).

When Einstein's Theory is analyzed in its—very—basic principles, as has been done above, the influence of the C-K-H process in Einstein's theory becomes obvious. Physics—Newtonian and modern—itself is a largely *a priori* science, so the primacy of mind is a given, along with the use of mind to find truth by either doubting (disproving) or accepting as true (proving) given principles, and the application of true principles to obtain results (sometimes the results are *a priori*, and sometimes they are *a posteriori*, but all fit Kant's criteria of synthetic propositions); Descartes' and some of Kant's contributions are thus accounted for in modern physics. While Einstein's Theory revolutionized the science of physics, Einstein's physics is bound just as tightly—if not more so—to the C-K-H process as classical (Newtonian) physics ever was. Indeed, the equivalence of opposites—a concept pioneered by Hegel—is fundamental to Einstein's Theory of Relativity[8], and was nowhere present in classical physics, which would seem to tie Einstein's physics more closely to the C-K-H process than classical physics was. The Theory of Relativity, in both its forms, employs the *reduction* of all phenomena into "two very heterogeneous elements"[9], specifically the observer and the observed, obtaining the *synthesis* of observation (apparent phenomena) by their interaction, with the corollary that the observed and observer are interchangeable. This accounts for the remainder of Kant's and for Hegel's contributions. This process of reduction-and-synthesis can also very clearly be seen in Einstein's most famous extrapolation from his Theory, where he reduces the number of underlying laws of physics by the expedient of synthesizing two of the laws (the Conservation of Energy and Mass) into one law, expressed as $E=mc^2$.

But the synthesis of physics did not stop with Einstein.

Noted above was the fact that Einstein's Theory of Relativity is one of two pillars of modern physics. The second pillar, which we will briefly discuss now, is quantum mechanics. While the Theory of Relativity has helped physicists to understand the vastly larger universe that surrounds us—that of stars, planets, and galaxies—quantum mechanics is the framework physicists use to understand behavior of the universe on the smallest of scales, that of subatomic particles (those units of matter that are smaller than atoms).

According to quantum mechanics, subatomic particles—whether on their own or as part of an atom—simultaneously behave as a particle (an individual unit of matter, like any single physical object) and as a wave (an observable pattern of force, such as a ripple in water or a sound). Although this defies common sense, it has been verified by numerous experiments[10]. To compound the confusion, there is Heisenberg's Uncertainty Principle, presented by Werner Heisenberg in 1927; in essence, this principle states that a specific subatomic particle's position or that specific subatomic particle's velocity can be known, but not both at the same time. Furthermore, the more exact of an observation is made of one quality, the less exact of an assessment is possible of the other[11]. As a subatomic particle moves—and there is no such thing as a stationary subatomic particle, even as part of an atom—it moves through *all possible trajectories at the same time*, with all trajectories but one cancelling each other out; this set of all possible trajectories for a given particle is called the particle's *probability wave*, because while a subatomic particle's trajectory is never one hundred percent predictable, certain trajectories are more probably than others. The trajectory a subatomic particle observably ("actually") takes therefore obtains one hundred percent probability, reducing the probability of all other trajectories to zero[12]. According to the physicist Richard Feynman, the reason Newtonian physics works in the everyday world, is because multiple subatomic particles' probability waves (such as in an atom or in any collection of atoms) cancel each other out, and create a certainty that corresponds to Newton's Laws of Motion at the atomic level and larger[13].

Also according to Feynman, there is no way to observe phenomena on the subatomic level without affecting the phenomena being observed[14]. In this, along with the dominance of probability in subatomic phenomena, we find the reduction-and-synthesis process outlined in the Theory of Relativity to be fundamental in quantum mechanics as well (that of reduction to the observed-observer duality, the synthesis of which produces observation). On the subatomic level, this is expressed by Feynman's observation that we cannot observe subatomic phenomena without affecting the phenomenon being observed. On the atomic and larger level, this is expressed in the fact that a probability regarding any phenomena never becomes a certainty, until an observer is introduced; a good example of this is the well-known Schroedinger's Cat analogy, where a cat is placed in a box with a (cat-proof) capsule of poison gas, said capsule having exactly a fifty percent chance of shattering—and thereby killing the cat—at any given time. So the question is, when not being observed, is the cat alive, dead, or neither. The answer is "indeterminate"; there is no meaningful answer to the question, until someone opens the box and acts as an "observer" of the cat's fate, changing the probability of the cat's life (or death) into a certainty.

The process of synthesis in the field of theoretical physics is ongoing. While the Theory of Relativity and quantum mechanics are each wonderful tools that produce incredible results in different areas, there is a problem: they are fundamentally incompatible. Essentially, the problem is gravity. As a field of force, gravity is probably made up of subatomic particles; while physicists haven't yet isolated a graviton (a basic unit of gravity) the fact that the other three "fundamental forces" that physicists know of—electromagnetism, the strong nuclear force, and the weak nuclear force—have corresponding fundamental subatomic particles (photons for electromagnetism, gluons for the strong atomic force, and certain bosons for the weak atomic force), and the fact that gravity seems to follow similar laws to the other fundamental forces, provides circumstantial evidence for the existence of gravitons. Problems arise because the Theory of Relativity depends upon certainty; while observations can be relative to each other, space and time must have a certain shape (any shape as long as it is certain) so that the relativity of observations can be accounted for. Space and time are shaped by gravity, so in order for space and time to have certainty, gravity must have certainty. But according to quantum mechanics, at the subatomic level where the fundamental forces are defined (including gravity) there is no certainty, only probability. This means that space has no certain shape, which renders all findings of the Theory of Relativity as "probable" rather than "certain". This would seem to disprove both theories (Relativity and QM), except for the fact they are both so accurate in their specific areas; the paradox only occurs when an attempt is made to combine—synthesize—the two theories to describe a given phenomenon (gravity being the prime example). This has led physicists to conclude that neither theory is wrong, merely that both are incomplete; an underlying theory of the two—a general synthesis—is now being sought. Over the course of the 20th Century, physicists have synthesized each of the other three fundamental forces with the Theory of Relativity through the studies of quantum electrodynamics, quantum chromodynamics, and quantum electroweak theory, collectively called "quantum field theory," comprising the "standard model" of modern physics. At the dawn of the 21st Century there are now several different theories attempting to unify (or, synthesize) all of quantum field theory with gravity: superstring theory, twistor theory, and the new variable method[15]. This continuing attempt to reduce-and-synthesize demonstrates the continuing influence of the C-K-H process in theoretical physics up to the present day.

And finally, even the future of physics is being shaped by the C-K-H process. One of the most significant conclusions of superstring theory (the current front-runner in the race for grand unification in physics), is that while physicists believe space-time is expanding, we can't know for sure because—if superstring theory is correct—*expansion and contraction of space-time looks exactly the same.* The reason we perceive space-time to be expanding, is because we only have one way to measure space-time's movement, in the form of photons, which are very light-weight particles. If we were able to measure other, extremely heavy subatomic particles which physicists theorize must exist but that we don't currently have the technology to verify, it is a theoretical near-certainty that we would obtain measurements indicating that space-time is contracting. And, according to superstring theory, both of these seemingly contradictory statements would be correct; the realities each conclusion describes would be indistinguishable from each other (the laws of physics would remain constant, and distances would appear unchanged), and so contraction and expansion of space-time becomes a difference in perception rather than a difference in physics. Also according to superstring theory, there wouldn't even be a "Big Crunch" (an event where space-time contracts to a single point measuring zero, a definite indicator of the contraction of space-time) in a contracting universe, because the "strings" that make up subatomic particles would force the universe back into expansion once a certain amount of contraction had been reached, a "Big Bounce" replacing a "Big Crunch". This is a perfect example of reducing a phenomenon—the measure of space-time—to two opposites (the motion of expansion and the motion of contraction), which when recombined with the observer's perception perfectly recreates the stated phenomenon, showing as a corollary that the two opposites comprising the described phenomenon are not only equal, but in the final analysis are the same thing. Once again, we have the universe described by the doubting mind put forward by Descartes, obtaining its true principles through the reduction and synthesis described by Kant, along with Hegel's conclusion of the equivalence of opposites. For a more complete (but still easily readable for the non-physicist) description of the theoretical conclusions of superstring theory touched on here, the reader is referred to Brian Greene's book "The Elegant Universe," pp239-54.

Of course, one might conclude that it is logical and appropriate that philosophies so admiring of mathematics as those of Descartes and Kant, if valid, would later come to underpin advances in other studies so closely associated with mathematics, such as physics. But what if we look into areas of study far outside the mathematically-described realms of physics, and find these other areas just as beholden to the same philosophical structure?

The 20th Century's New Science

While all other areas of study discussed in this chapter experienced innovations in the 20th Century, psychology stands alone in being itself an innovation of the 20th Century. As we will show in this section, many of the fundamental discoveries of psychology (and perhaps even the field of psychology itself, as we currently understand it) are not available to a mind or a culture not grounded in the C-K-H process.

While the roots of the study of psychology lie in the fields of religion, philosophy, and neuroscience, psychoanalysis—arguably the innovation that irrevocably differentiated psychology from other fields of study—could be said to have been born with the 20th Century, in the year 1900, with the publication of Sigmund Freud's book "The Interpretation of Dreams". This book was revolutionary, not only because it proposed a systematic way of interpreting dreams that was verifiable by experience (unlike other methods of dream interpretation used previously), but because in it Freud suggested the existence of the "unconscious mind"; an integral part of the human psyche that is a source of motivation, yet whose workings (and even existence) are completely invisible to the untrained conscious mind. This idea was anathema to the wisdom of the time, which held that "mind" and "consciousness" required each other to exist. Freud's conception eventually won out, and now, the "unconscious mind" suggested by Freud in his first major work (and which was to continue to figure prominently in his work, as well as help define the field of psychology as distinct from any other study of human consciousness) continues to occupy the attention of psychology and psychologists to the present day under the label of the "subconscious".

While much of Freud's work continues to be very influential in the field of psychology—and provides along the way many excellent examples of the C-K-H process' influence—this section will focus on one of Freud's later, but most influential, works, "The Ego and the Id," for the purpose of illustration. Published in 1923, this short book is where Freud definitively laid out his ideas not only on the divisions that exist in the human mind (the dichotomy between the conscious and unconscious, the id, the ego, the super-ego/"ego ideal", and the id/ego/super-ego's level of submersion in the unconscious), but also on the basic drives that motivate human behavior (the pleasure principle, the sex-drive, the death instinct, and the Oedipus complex). These fundamental ideas will be examined briefly below by summarizing the chapters of Freud's book. This will illustrate how Freud's formulation of the human psyche is indelibly shaped by the C-K-H process.

In the first chapter of "The Ego and the Id," Freud once again makes the case for the reality of unconscious thought[16], and states that the purpose of psychoanalysis is to make more of the unconscious processes conscious[17]. He also points out that the ego—the apparent seat of the conscious mind—has part of itself submerged in the unconscious, which is the explanation for the sublimation of unacceptable promptings emanating from the id (also called "repressions")[18]. As Freud states at the end of the first chapter, "for the property of being conscious or not is in the last resort our one beacon-light in the darkness of depth-psychology."[19].

In the second chapter, Freud delineates the differences between the ego and the id, and how both have parts of themselves submerged in the unconscious. Freud states here that while the id is shaped by instinct, the ego is shaped by perceptions[20], which brings the two of them into conflict (the ego repressing unacceptable drives, as discussed in the first chapter, as well as trying to bring the id in line with the "reality principle" rather than the "pleasure principle" by which the id naturally operates[21]).

The third chapter describes the relationship between the ego and the super-ego; essentially the super-ego is the sum of those earliest "emotional cathexes" which originally formed the ego, and towards which the ego constantly strives, while at the same time the super-ego resides significantly more in the unconscious than the ego does[22]. Also in this chapter, Freud describes the existence of a dual Oedipus complex in each individual (a son not only desires his mother and is jealous of his father, but also desires his father and is jealous of his mother; vice versa for daughters), the resolution of which determines the amount of apparent bisexuality ("ambivalence") in the adult individual[23].

The fourth chapter is where Freud categorizes the basic instincts that drive the individual, and explains where the power behind these drives comes from. Freud classifies all instincts as belonging either to the sexual instinct, or the death instinct[24]. These two sets of instincts, in addition to motivating the individual separately, often blend together to create certain behaviors (such as sexual sadism)[25]. Both categories of instinct have access to a "displaceable energy" within the psyche; whichever class of instinct is given more access to this "displaceable energy" is the one that motivates behavior, and Freud gives examples of this[26]. Freud also describes *libido* as the "displaceable" energy the id and the ego compete with each other for (sexualized libido in the case of the id, desexualized libido in the case of the ego[27]) as well as the consequence of this being that the ego, in competing with the id for this energy (which originally emanates from the id), must pay for its victories by serving the id in other ways[28].

In the fifth and final chapter of "The Ego and the Id," Freud elaborates further on the "dependent relationships"[29] that define the ego: ego/id, ego/super-ego, and ego/perception. These relationships can be called "dependent" because while the ego stands in apparent opposition to these other entities, the ego's interaction with these entities is often what defines the ego and give the ego its components; the ego is therefore "dependent" upon them for its very existence. Indeed, Freud points out in multiple places (previous to the fifth chapter) that while the ego and id appear to be separate, the ego is merely a differentiation of the id, its choices often dictated by instinctual drives despite its apparent attempts to "tame" those same drives[30]. In addition to this, it becomes evident upon close examination that the super-ego—the seat of what is generally considered "morality"[31], and so logically the opposite of the amoral id[32]—instead of being the ally of the ego against the id, usually works for the id against the ego, having originated in the id and remaining (like the id) mostly in the realm of the unconscious[33]. In fact, it becomes clear that the defining feature of the "relationship" between the ego and the super-ego is the ego's struggle for self-preservation against the super-ego's onslaught of death-instinct[34]. And finally, although experiences from the world of outside (external) perception enrich the ego (and give it the means of "reality-testing" the id's instinctual drives), it has another "outside" world to contend with, that of internal perception, which is dictated by the id and which the id uses to great effect, to suborn the ego to its (the id's) wishes[35].

The C-K-H process becomes evident on multiple levels, once the description of Freud's analytical tools is stripped of its clinical examples. The echo of Descartes' "I think, therefore I am" can easily be heard in Freud's premise of consciousness being "our one beacon-light in the darkness of depth-psychology," along with the Cartesian principles of doubt, and the premise that un-doubtable principles are true, being embodied in the very fabric of psychoanalysis (bringing the perception of real unconscious processes to consciousness, thereby giving more power to the conscious mind). With these principles firmly established, Freud goes on to demonstrate the reduction-and-synthesis process through the reduction-to-dualities of conscious/unconscious, sex-instinct/death-instinct, sexualized libido/de-sexualized libido, male Oedipus complex/female Oedipus complex, ego/id, ego/super-ego, and external perception/internal perception. All of these are recognizable as equivalent opposites, and all are demonstrably capable of synthesis.

Freud's work (as well as that of Jung, Klein, Ericson and many others in the field) contains numerous other examples of C-K-H influence, but the examples shown here should be sufficient for the purpose of illustration. While some of Freud's conclusions have been disputed over the course of the 20th Century, the science of psychology still operates within the framework (and using much of the vocabulary) originally developed by Freud. The very field of psychology, as it is widely understood in the early 21st century, would not exist without the assumption of an "unconscious mind," and very few (if any) psychologists today dispute the existence of the id, ego and super-ego. None of these dualities Freud described, or their dynamic relationships, is apprehensible without the observing mind being thoroughly grounded in the C-K-H process.

It seems somewhat ironic, that philosophical principles divorced from clinical trial have had such an influence on the science of psychology. Much of the first chapter of "The Ego and the Id," where Freud is making the case for the reality of the unconscious mind, is written to counter the objections the "philosophy" and "philosophers" of his time raised against his arguments[36]. In some ways, psychology has supplanted philosophy over the course of the 20th Century, answering basic questions of human perception and the human cognitive process in a much more satisfying way than philosophy ever has. However, in view of the apparent influence of the C-K-H process (a philosophical construct) on the science of psychology, perhaps what has happened isn't so much a supplanting of philosophy with a science, as a further synthesis of philosophy with the scientific method, blurring once again the distinction between science and philosophy that scientists of the 20th Century (such as Freud) worked so hard to create. Freud's attempt to separate philosophy from science was undermined by his own unconscious adherence to a philosophical process. Not only did the C-K-H process evidently shape Freud's thinking in formulating his theories, but the general acceptance of the C-K-H process by the dawn of the 20th Century gave Freud's contemporaries—and us—the framework upon which these theories can be understood.

Psychology is, among other things, a study of individual human behavior. It has been shown in this section how the C-K-H process has influenced the foundation of this study greatly. The next section examines how this process has applied to human behavior on a more collective level over the course of the 20th Century.

Calculating the Cost

Of all the sciences, economics—even more so than physics—lends itself most thoroughly to the C-K-H process. Ever since economics' birth as a science with the publication of Adam Smith's work "An Inquiry Into The Nature And Causes Of The Wealth Of Nations" in 1776 (usually known nowadays simply as "The Wealth of Nations"), almost every basic term of economics could be described as an interplay of opposites creating a dynamic synthesis. Examples of this include the theories of value, wages, prices, costs, interest rates and the "business cycle"; while an analysis of these terms would be instructive, it is too lengthy of a task to attempt here. In this section, we will confine ourselves to discussing some of the ideas and "innovations" of the 20th Century's most influential economist—John Maynard Keynes—as well as some contributions by the second most influential, Milton Freidman, the influence of the C-K-H process on their contributions, and the efficacy (or lack thereof) of these contributions when applied to the world of experience.

In 1935, John Maynard Keynes published what was to become his masterpiece, "The General Theory of Employment, Interest, and Money" in answer to The Great Depression afflicting the world at that time. While agreeing with "classical" economics (which Keynes defined as the economic theory expressed in the works of Ricardo, Marshall, Edgeworth, and Pigou[37]) up to a point, Keynes felt that the exclusion of *effective demand* made the classical theories inapplicable to the real world, as evidenced by their inability to forecast economic conditions[38]. According to Keynes, *effective demand* is the intersection (synthesis) of aggregate—i.e. total—demand and aggregate supply in a given economy[39]; according to Keynes, increasing *effective demand* by increasing aggregate consumption would increase employment in a given society, up to as close to zero unemployment as is possible[40]. Keynes states that the way to increase *effective demand* is to lower interest rates, which encourages borrowing, which in turn encourages spending (i.e. consumption), and this increased consumption then increases *effective demand*. According to Keynes, this not only raises the employment level to as near zero as is possible, but guarantees that supply increases in lockstep with demand; as long as *effective demand* remains high, and interest rates remain low, supply cannot fail to keep up with demand, making demand (i.e. consumption) the true driving force in any economy. It was Keynes' emphasis on "supply and demand"—especially "demand"—that has made these three words a staple of economic discourse in the 20th Century. According to Keynes, the reason theories of "classical" economics could not match up to the world of experience, was because these theories underestimated the importance of demand in an economy; the classical theories taught that supply produced demand in an economy, rather than demand producing supply, and therefore the classical theories placed an unnecessary and even harmful emphasis on saving money, along with fostering other dangerous delusions about interest rates, the nature of money and employment, and the overall justice of a free market[41]. In fact, Keynes goes so far as to suggest that not only are the *propensity to consume* (i.e. demand) and the *propensity to save/invest* (i.e. supply) the two necessary elements in discovering *effective demand* (and therefore in analyzing a given economy), but in fact these two elements are interchangeable, with the final analysis revealing them both as a propensity to consume[42].

This process of reduction-and-synthesis evident in Keynes' exposition of *effective demand*, where a phenomenon (i.e. *effective demand*) is understood as the interplay of two opposites (i.e. supply and demand) and these opposites, in the final analysis, are shown to be equivalent, should be very familiar to us by now.

As we have discovered over the course of the 20th Century, Keynes' ideas work about as well as the "classical" ideas in predicting the behavior of an economy; in other words, they don't work reliably. According to Keynesian theory, the Japanese economic boom of the 1980's and that of the United States in the 1990's should have been sustainable indefinitely as long as interest rates were kept low (which they were); we have discovered, *a posteriori*, that these economic bubbles burst nonetheless. In fact, as Japan has demonstrated over the last twenty years by its rigorous application of Keynesian principles to revive its economy and having singularly failed to do so, Keynesian theory is sometimes simply wrong. The same has happened in the United States, after its boom in the late '90's; although the economy in early 2011 is said to have improved since the banking and real-estate crises of 2008, it is quite fragile, and very few outside the industries of banking, insurance, and government in the U.S. could state that they are more prosperous in 2011 than they were in 1999. Applications of Keynesian principles to stimulate the economy have failed to bring back the boom (not that we should have to "bring back the boom" at all; Keynesian principles were applied liberally during the boom, which according to Keynesian theory should have sustained the boom indefinitely). As inviting as Keynes' *a priori* model is, it does not reflect real-world behavior. Here is why.

In the case of Japan, low interest rates and other encouragements to consume have failed to increase consumption. There are several theories about why this is so—such as an aging population, an ingrained desire to save, an unwillingness to change status-conscious behavior—but the fact is that Keynes' ideas have failed when applied to Japan and its culture. They have failed in the United States as well, but (perhaps because the United States has a culture closer to that of the English Keynes) the reasons are more easily explainable in Keynes' own terminology.

In Chapter 2, Section II, paragraph 2 of The General Theory, Keynes makes the statement "The psychology of the community is such that when aggregate real income is increased, aggregate consumption is increased, but not so much as income." So according to Keynes, if a group of individuals obtain a total of an extra million dollars of income in a year, their total spending will increase that year by an amount less than a million dollars. While this may seem intuitively obvious, when applied to a society already saturated in

Keynesian thinking it is inapplicable; in such as society—such as early 21st Century America—when aggregate real income is increased, aggregate consumption increases *more than the increase in income*. There are several reasons for this: Easy credit, the low interest rates that foster easy credit, a tax structure that encourages debt, the perceived uselessness of saving, and the perceived need to consume.

In 2004, almost anyone over the age of 18 could obtain a credit card or a bank loan. While credit cards can carry very high interest rates (9-18% accrued per month), most credit card holders are allowed to make a "minimum payment"—paying only the interest accrued that month on the debt attached to that card—rather than paying off the total balance every month. This allows credit card holders to carry outstanding balances (i.e. unpaid debts) on their credit cards indefinitely. More purchases can be made using most credit cards as long as these "minimum payments" are made, increasing the balance (and the minimum payment, of course). Consumer loans, car loans, school loans, business loans, and especially mortgage loans were not much more difficult to procure, and carried a lower interest rate; while there was a definite expectation that the principal of these loans would eventually be repaid (payment on the loan's principal being factored into the monthly loan repayment schedule), the fact that all interest paid on certain kinds of loans—such as those for school, business, and home—are tax deductible, and that a history of reliably making payments on any kind of loan (a "credit history") makes larger sums of money available to be borrowed at lower interest rates, encouraged the general public to go deeply into debt. The upshot of all this is that an American consumer could easily borrow more money than he or she could ever pay off; the debtor's financial responsibility was widely held to be payment only of the interest, rather than of both interest and principal, in most cases. Experience has shown that in this situation a consumer's spending habits do not grow to match their income, but grow to match their credit limit (a number often multiples of their income). If members of the general public—often called "consumers" in early 21st Century economic parlance—were reluctant to spend and go into debt to their credit limit, they received further encouragement to do so in the perceived uselessness of saving and the perceived "need" to consume. With interest rates kept low by a central bank to encourage debt and consumption, the rate of return on most financial investments such as savings accounts, stock dividends and bonds was below the rate of inflation (the rate at which the supply of currency increases), and so the purchasing power of any money put into savings quickly eroded. As an example, if $1,000 is put into a savings account with an interest rate of 1% per year (and there are no deposits or withdrawals to the account during that year), while the rate of inflation (the rate at which the total number of U.S. dollars in the world increases) is at 3% per year, though the number of the dollars in the account increases to $1,010 after a year's time, the purchasing power of those dollars is actually only equivalent to $980—the money has lost 2% of its original purchasing power. So, when the interest rate is lower than the inflation rate, there is no way to save money that preserves its purchasing power. Therefore, money not spent immediately loses its purchasing power, while debt appears easier to repay the longer one draws out the payments (fixed amounts of money become "cheaper," or easier to obtain, over time during inflation). On top of this, consumers were taught that this combination of un-payable debt, low interest rates, and inflation, was a good thing through their schooling, public pronouncements by central bankers (Federal Reserve officials, in the U.S.), and investment counselors; the party line was that as long consumers were able to consume, everyone could stay employed and consuming, and so saving was unnecessary and even harmful. If currency was needed, so the popular wisdom went, it could be borrowed.

Immediately after the sentence quoted above from Keynes' General Theory, Keynes states "Hence employers would make a loss if the whole of the increased employment of capital were to be devoted to satisfying the increased demand for immediate consumption." In other words, if a group of people gained an extra million dollars, and the entire million dollars was consumed (spent or destroyed, rather than saved or invested), employers would lose money, they would decrease their output—and lay off employees— and the general level of wealth and employment would decline instead of increase. Employing capital to pay down un-payable debts is proving equivalent to consumption, not to saving or investment. Due to policies implemented to encourage *effective demand* (e.g. keeping the rate of inflation higher than the rate of interest, giving tax breaks for going into debt, publicly encouraging consumers to borrow and spend), combined with Keynes himself giving the academic green light to unlimited consumption by dissolving the difference between consumption and saving/investment[43], we have gone beyond the negative scenario envisioned by Keynes; aggregate consumption has not increased as fast as aggregate income has, it has increased *faster*, and continues to do so. In a rare agreement between Keynes and common sense, this is a recipe for disaster. This explains why debt is still so crippling, bankruptcy on all levels is increasingly common, and net worth ("wealth" as measured by a positive ratio of assets to liabilities) generally continues to decrease, despite supposed "austerity measures" taken on both the personal and collective level in many nations.

In 2011, the truth of this was sadly apparent. While unemployment grew significantly from 2004, credit became harder to come by. Although the mindset of many market actors regarding their finances altered between 2004 and 2011, very little of meaningful change occurred. Most kinds of loans were somewhat harder for the average U.S. citizen to obtain in 2011 than they were in 2004, but the financial incentives in place and the negative net worth of most market actors (and the habits that perpetuated this state of affairs) did not change in any meaningful way. Most individuals and institutions in America in 2011 still had far more debt than they could ever pay off, and still continued to live beyond their means (trusting to government subsidies or helpful family members, rather than bank-issued credit, to make up the difference). Though the level of consumption fell in many markets, low interest rates and huge debts prevented capital from flowing freely toward saving and investment.

The most noticeable difference between 2004 and 2011 seems to have been one of emphasis. The attitude of economic actors shifted in that time (especially after 2008), from a focus on greed to a focus on fear. Whereas in 2004 many were willing to spend every penny they had—and more—for immediate gratification, in 2011 much of the disposable income people had (including much of the subsidies from family members and various levels of government) went toward paying down debt, rather than toward savings, new consumption, or investment. Those institutions that still borrowed heavily—such as government and the banking industry—actually increased the rate at which they borrowed, both from taxpayers and from each other, but for the purpose of sustaining what they had already begun or maintaining what they have already acquired, rather than actually beginning or acquiring anything new. They appeared to be running as hard as they could just to stay in place.

Unfortunately, while this overall shift from greed to fear should theoretically have been a good thing, as market actors lowered their levels of consumption for the purpose of shifting capital toward saving and investment, other circumstances have prevented these necessary shifts of capital from being completed. At all levels, the majority of debts owed and held remained effectively un-payable, and so the payments made toward them—whether on the interest or the principle—were wasted. Universally, debtors in the early 21st Century have no real chance of ever paying down the principle of their debts, and creditors are almost certain to lose the majority of capital they've put into purchasing bonds, derivatives and other debt-instruments. Although many people believe they are consuming less, all capital put toward paying down debt is effectively destroyed (i.e. permanently removed from the financial system), since it is not being saved or invested by themselves or their creditors. When debtors pay creditors part of what is owed, the capital used to make this payment is not being saved or invested directly by the debtor. This is supposedly a task for the creditors, a task that creditors are unable or unwilling to undertake in the early 21st Century. Instead, creditors are taking the capital they collect from debt repayment and either purchasing more debt from others in the form of bonds or derivatives, or are using this capital as leverage to issue more of their own bonds or derivatives. Neither of these uses constitutes actual saving or investment on the part of the creditor.

The capital destruction inherent to all this activity is having the same effect as what is normally termed "consumption" (i.e. the use of capital to purchase goods or services) would. Even though *effective demand* for goods and services is reduced, the effective level of consumption (i.e. the amount of capital spent on something other than saving or investment) has not really been reduced at all. It may have even increased. This means that the rate of effective consumption in 2011 still outpaced income. The outpacing of income by consumption prevents capital formation, and in fact continues to destroy capital at an alarming rate. Capital that was shifted away from consumption between 2008 and 2011 never completed its much-needed move into savings or investments. Rather, it was diverted into debt-repayment, where it was destroyed. If capital cannot complete its shift away from consumption and into savings and investments, then the savings and investment that support consumption cannot be sustained. This state of affairs ensures chronic undercapitalization, domino-style default, and high unemployment.

The situation at the beginning of 2012 is far from lost, but drastic measures appear to be called for. All debt carried by insolvent borrowers must be written off, regardless of why it was acquired, who acquired it, or who it is owed to. Realistic accounting standards must be re-instituted and enforced for all market actors, insisting on a "mark-to-market" rather than "mark-to-model" evaluation of assets. Individuals and institutions must be expected to live within their means, and not be protected when they fail to do so. People, institutions, and governments who are rendered insolvent by debt-forgiveness (i.e. those whose solvency depends on the repayment of unsupportable debt by others) must be allowed to go bankrupt. Tax breaks encouraging debt-repayment have to be ended. Interest rates must be allowed to rise to match inflation—or currencies must deflate to match low interest rates. Mainstream economic theorists must open their eyes to the *a posteriori* results of the application their *a priori* models, and learn to modify their models accordingly, or be drummed out of their profession. Unless all these things are done, the ongoing period of economic decline is likely to continue into 2012 and beyond.

The application of Keynesian principles to stimulate consumption/demand, along with acceptance of these principles by the general population, clearly alters the "psychology of the community" Keynes referred to, and so alters the applicability of Keynes' General Theory.

Keynes' General Theory is a prominent example—though unfortunately not the only one—of how the application of the C-K-H process can go, and has gone, horribly wrong. As Kant points out in the Critique of Pure Reason, pure reason (obtained by use of the C-K-H process) is only capable of ascertaining negative truth. It can prove something is false; it cannot assert positive truth (it cannot prove that a statement is true) without experiential verification[44]. Keynes attempted, with his General Theory, to assert positive *a priori* truth *without* experiential verification. The results, though long-delayed, are proving disastrous, while asserting the C-K-H process' ubiquitous influence.

Up to this point, the origin and nature of the C-K-H process has been examined and examples have been cited of how this process has been applied to increase our understanding in areas outside of philosophy. Part of the purpose of this section is to show another potential result of the application of this process: that it is equally capable of decreasing our general understanding when misapplied. While Keynes' theory has led a great many people to temporary prosperity, it seems to have done so at the expense of long-term financial security. Indeed, if Japan's 20-year depression—created and sustained by strictly Keynesian policies—is any indication, Keynes' cure for The Great Depression (which lasted 12 years in the U.S.) is worse than the disease. The economic malaise in the United States—ongoing for 3 years at the time of this writing—may prove to be yet another cautionary tale.

While Keynes' General Theory is inconsistent with the real world, it is at least consistent with its own principles. The same cannot be said, unfortunately, for the thinking of the other great economist of the 20th Century, Milton Friedman. Not only does Friedman's economic philosophy appear inapplicable to the real world, it is glaringly self-contradictory; yet its presentation has given it a veneer of plausibility to minds shaped by the C-K-H process.

In his book "Capitalism and Freedom" published in 1962, written based on a series of lectures he delivered in 1956, Friedman outlines his theory of economics. In the first two chapters, Friedman delineates the essential opposition between the free market and government control: the free market always produces greater overall prosperity and individual freedom, while government control always leads to less prosperity for all and the restriction of personal freedom. This is what Friedman terms the "19th Century liberal" outlook, and calls himself a "liberal" by that definition. The next ten chapters are examinations of different areas of socioeconomic activity, with thoughts on how they could be improved by the application of Friedman's "liberal" economic philosophy. There are two problems: the first is that Friedman goes against his own "liberal" principles on six issues out of ten[45], proposing changes to existing government regulation rather than reducing or eliminating the regulation. For example, in regards to the regulation of money[46], he shows that while the central banks of various nations have never been able to produce a stable currency, the free market's preference for a commodities-based standard hasn't been particularly stable either; Friedman's solution is to *have government regulate the interest paid on the money produced by a central bank to a certain small rise per year*. This "liberal" solution, where it seems a compromise is sought between the stability of a commodity-based currency and the ready availability of fiat currency, sounds much more like a 20th Century liberal (favoring government control rather than free markets) rather than the 19th Century liberal Friedman claims to be, since it does not suggest reducing or eliminating government control at all. While his solution may, at first blush, appear to be a synthesis of opposites (and hence appealing to the C-K-H-steeped 20th Century mind) it is fundamentally self-contradictory, in that the opposites of government control and free-market control, according to Friedman himself, are not equivalent; one (free market control) is always preferable to the other (government control)[47], and therefore logically the preferable (i.e. free-market) should always be encouraged while the less preferable (government regulation) should always be done away with. Yet despite this logical necessity of preferring free-market control, Friedman's suggestions are often simply cosmetic modifications of existing government control. According to Friedman's own professed "liberal" principles, his suggestions should lead to decreased freedom and reduced prosperity, the opposite of his stated intention.

In his defense, Friedman himself states that that government is not eliminated by adherence to "liberal" principles; only that, instead of being both player and referee in any given "game" (sociopolitical activity), government's role should be restricted to that of referee. This is still logically inconsistent, however, since it claims government control is simultaneously necessary to ensure freedom and prosperity, while its involvement also guarantees a reduction in freedom and prosperity (a necessary evil, as it were)[48]. This contradiction is supposed to be accepted on faith (see "Capitalism and Freedom" p194 for an example).

Friedman's logical inconsistencies might be forgiven if (like Kant's) his suggestions had their intended effect when implemented. This does not seem to be the case. Central banks that have tried to follow Friedman's suggestion of a carefully measured annual rise in interest rates have all sooner or later, without exception, given in to greed and political pressure to change their stance. The United States federal government (along with every other government on the planet) has followed all of Friedman's suggestions for creating a free market in gold and foreign exchange: allowing the national currency to float relative to gold and to other national currencies, divesting the government of its stocks of gold, allowing citizens to hold gold in commodity form or as part of a financial instrument, successfully pressuring the IMF to accept the lack of a fixed value for the dollar, and allowing other nations to use the dollar as a reserve currency[49]. On page 71 of Capitalism and Freedom, Friedman said: *A system such as that just outlined would solve the balance of payments problem once and for all. No deficit could possibly arise to require high government officials to plead with foreign countries and central banks for assistance, or to require an American President to behave like a harried country banker trying to restore confidence in his bank, or to force an administration preaching free trade to impose import restrictions, or to sacrifice important national and personal interests to the trivial question of the name of the currency in which payments are made.* While there is now arguably a free market in gold, and it's true in 2011 that there is no question that U.S. dollars are supposed to be used to pay off U.S. debts, none of the other promised benefits of this system appear to have come true, for the U.S. or for any of the other governments that embraced Friedman's suggestions. Current estimates of the U.S. federal deficit range from $8 trillion to $44 trillion. This has caused much talk in Congress in recent years about the "unfair" economic practices of China (especially regarding its peg to the U.S. dollar), caused countries such as China, Russia, and Brazil to question the usefulness of the dollar as a reserve currency, and caused the Federal Reserve to institute two official (and a third unofficial) "quantitative easing" programs to the tune of trillions of dollars, in order to maintain confidence in the market for U.S. Treasury bonds. In late 2009, the Obama administration imposed punitive tariffs on tires imported from China at the behest of U.S. union United Steelworkers, when earlier in his Presidency he had criticized other countries for practicing protectionism. Other countries that have followed these suggestions of Friedman's over the last forty years—Malaysia, South Korea, Russia, Argentina, and most recently Greece and Ireland—have had to "plead with foreign countries and central banks for assistance" because of the unsupportable national deficits created as a direct result of following these suggestions.

All this makes Friedman's track record appear very poor. Some other suggestions that Friedman has made—such as removing the postal monopoly held by the U.S. Postal Service—remain untried, but appear so impractical and politically unpalatable that they are likely to remain untried indefinitely.

So how did these inconsistent and demonstrably inaccurate philosophies become (and remain) the mainstays of one of the most important sciences of the 20th Century? Partly, it was due to whom the philosophies benefited. Both philosophies assumed the existence of a central bank with absolute control over a nation's currency, which gave a lot of power (and so inevitably appealed) to politicians and bankers. Also, both are difficult to follow without "technical" training—especially Keynes—which guaranteed jobs and status for economics professors and those in the financial industry. In addition, these philosophies appeal to the general public, by telling a majority of people what they want to hear (e.g. government policy can make unlimited spending OK). The fact that the general public swallowed these philosophies whole, and largely continues to do so even when they fail to predict problems or to fix them when they arise, is a sad tribute to the influence of the C-K-H process on thought outside of academia and politics; because both Keynes' and Friedman's economic systems present opposites (and are even presented at times as opposites of each other!), and then present a reasonable-sounding way to bring these opposites to synthesis, they are given a patina of plausibility in the minds of the general public ("reasonable sounding" and "plausible" because a synthesis of equivalent opposites has become the form the best solutions are expected to take) and are accepted as true even when experience contradicts them.

It was stated above that economics was one of the most important sciences of the 20th Century; this was so, not only because of its impact on day-to-day life, but because the century's major worldwide struggle was between capitalism (representing "liberal" free market principles) and communism (the absolute control of all economic activity by government). This was essentially a difference of economic opinion, not what is usually thought of as a "political" opinion. The irony in the fact that the 20th Century's most influential champions of capitalism—Keynes and Friedman—espoused heavy market interventions (a form of socialism, and a step toward communism) has apparently been lost on most observers. This irony has been obscured by rhetoric, powerful interest groups, and a mistaken application of the C-K-H process on the part of the general public. It can be honestly stated that, at the beginning of the 21st Century, the citizens of the U.S. in particular (and the Westernized world in general) are actually less intelligent economically and less informed regarding economic influences that directly affect them, than citizens of same at the beginning of the 20th Century. This general ignorance and "dumbing down" of the populace can be attributed (at least in part) to the C-K-H process' application to economic thinking and education.

In the late 18th Century, economics was not a science in and of itself, but merely a branch of moral philosophy. Just as the differentiation of economics from philosophy, economics' use of the C-K-H process before the 20th Century, and economics' blind and ultimately destructive faith in the C-K-H process during the 20th Century has presaged what was to come in the society at large, the field of philosophy itself—as shown by its explication of the C-K-H process well before it became dominant in society—also may be a bellwether of what is to come. In the next section, we will see what results the C-K-H process has produced in the field of philosophy during the 20th Century, and what kind of future this may be indicating.

Deconstructing Meaning

"Post-modern" (also known as "pomo" or "post-structuralism"), has become a common adjective when referring to recent thought, literature, and art. The fact that very few people have a clear understanding of what, exactly, "post-modern" means or what "post-modernism" is doesn't seem to prevent its usage (this usage-without-understanding is itself very pomo, as will become evident). This section will describe pomo philosophy briefly, name its major proponents, show how it derived from the C-K-H process, take a look at one of its additions to 21st Century society in the U.S., and provide a brief analysis of its overall desirability.

Pomo philosophy is about language. The essential tenets of postmodern thought are:

#1: That all thought is made possible by language.
#2: All language is structured, and therefore all thought is structured by the language in which it is expressed.
#3: By recognizing the fact that all thought—and therefore everything we comprehend of the world we live in—has a structure, we are enabled to get outside the structure, critique it, and thereby use imagination/creativity to escape the structure's domination.

Pomo's major proponents are Martin Heidegger, Michel Foucault, and Jacques Derrida. While there are other philosophers that are considered post-modernist, these three men are the ones whose works appear to best represent and define the pomo paradigm.

Pomo is inherently deconstructionist; it requires a pre-existing system of thought and speech to function in, critique (deconstruct) and "escape." Heidegger, in his book "Introduction to Metaphysics" analyzed the meaning of the verb "to be," deduced that this verb is the root of all language (and therefore all thought and understanding), and concluded that no one since the pre-Socratic Greek philosophers Heraclitus and Parmenides have had functional definitions of this verb—and therefore no one since has been capable of accurately understanding or describing the world around them. Foucault, in his book "The Order of Things," described the metamorphosis of thought from the Renaissance to the late 19th Century not as an evolution, but as a series of random changes, in the mode of understanding, each new mode of understanding being essentially unrelated to and incompatible with the mode of understanding preceding it. The latest of these modes is the idea of "man" as a being that can objectively view the world around him; a mode that, in Foucault's opinion, is about to be supplanted by the next one. Since in Foucault's anti-teleology the idea of "man" defines the mode of the "modern" era, the next mode—and era—will of course be "post-modern;" hence the name of the philosophical school. Derrida…well, Derrida is so post-modern it's hard to tell if he has any meaning at all (at least in English; perhaps the structure of the English language is incompatible with the mode of understanding made possible by Derrida's native French). What is somewhat decipherable in Derrida's work is that he shares with Heidegger and Foucault the three tenets of pomo listed above, along with calls to action such as the following:

"Emancipation from this language [of form] must be attempted. But not as an *attempt* at emancipation from it, for this is impossible unless we forget *our* history. Rather, as the dream of emancipation. Nor as emancipation from it, which would be meaningless and deprive us of the light of meaning. Rather, as resistance to it, as far as is possible. In any event, we must not abandon ourselves to that language with the abandon which today characterizes the worst exhilaration of the most nuanced structural formalism. (italics in original)[50]

Which, to give Derrida credit, seems somewhat more clear than the calls to action—or lack thereof—trumpeted by Foucault and Heidegger. The fact that Derrida's call to action is completely meaningless (as are those made by Foucault and Heidegger) does not bother the advocates of pomo one little bit. The post-modernists, who all seem to admire Nietzsche, appear to think that this analysis and deconstruction of structure—*all* structure—is the manifestation of Nietzsche's "down-going," which will in turn produce "over-going," which in time will produce the Overman[51]. This, of course, makes a "structuralist" (i.e. meaningful) interpretation pointless, since the coming Overmen, as "post-modern" beings, won't be dependent on language or thought as we understand these terms, and will thereby not require any "structuralist" interpretation. The facts that the major proponents of post-modernism admit that they are not Overmen themselves[52], that no Overmen have been created by applying pomo, and that existing as a conscious being without utilizing some kind of structure for language and thought appears to be impossible, also don't seem to bother the advocates of pomo at all.

All this deconstructionism wouldn't be so bad, if the post-modernists could give humanity something to take the place of structure. Unfortunately they don't, and so pomo appears only able to exist as a parasite upon the very "structuralism" it claims to "escape". Heidegger's answer to the "question of being" he proposed was simply that the question must be continually re-asked; no criteria is given for what makes a functional answer to the question of being[53], other than that Heraclitus and Parmenides got it right once, and no one has gotten it right since. Foucault proposed that the result of the realization of structure (and limitation) of language was the creation of a self-referential literature to accompany the language[54], although he admitted that he had no idea what a world without man—or, if you will, a "post-modern" world—would or should look like[55]. Derrida—like Heidegger—calls on the writers of the world to bring the post-modern world into being (Heidegger called on artists and all other creators, as well[56]), but says only that the world they create should not look like the world we currently inhabit[57].

Unfortunately, this fixation on deconstructionism is not an aberration, but rather the logical progression of the C-K-H process, first applied by Nietzsche, when it is the only tool available for producing intellectual understanding (as has been the case throughout the 20th and early 21st Centuries). The principle laid down by Descartes of the supremacy of mind through its ability to doubt (and thereby understand) is quite evident in pomo. The C-K-H process of reduction-without-synthesis, implied by Kant and explored by Nietzsche, is quite evident as well (see Heidegger's definition of "being"[58] and Foucault's "analytic of finitude"[59]) in pomo's lack of an applicable synthesis of reduced elements and its proud self-justification of this lack. And Hegel's equivalence of opposites is quite evident[60], along with his arrogant dismissal of linearity and empiricism[61], not only in the writings of the postmodernists themselves, but also in their application by others. As already mentioned, *all* structure is equivalent in post-modernism, whatever its application or results. What this means in practical terms is that in post-modernism, Descartes' goal of discovering "true principles" is rendered impossible. Analysis and criticism of any structure is possible, but *nothing can be created to supplant the structure* since anything created would also be a structure, and so equivalent to the structure already analyzed and "escaped" from, requiring another analysis and another escape, *ad nauseum*. This state of affairs makes increases in understanding impossible. This insanity is what causes the philosophy of post-modernism to actually *reduce* the knowledge available to an individual immersed in it. Post-modernism goes beyond Nietzsche in deifying Kant's statement that only negative truth is attainable through pure reason, while at the same time disdaining Kant's insistence on experiential verification of *a priori* principles as mere "structuralism."

Like the economic theories discussed in the previous section, pomo is another example of how the C-K-H process can be misapplied. When misapplied, the C-K-H process reduces "true principles" and experiential phenomena to useless components or reasonable-sounding (but demonstrably unusable) syntheses. Pomo's deconstruction of knowledge doesn't appear to be making way for the Overman as the post-modernists hope, but is merely creating stupidity and chaos.

As an example of the stupidity and chaos being created, consider the "political correctness" cultural movement. A thoroughly pomo phenomena, PC seeks to change the way people think by altering language. In the 1950's, someone who couldn't walk was labeled as "lame" or "crippled." By the 1980's it was decided that the negative connotations of the words "lame" and "crippled" were adversely affecting the social consciousness (and the opportunities and self-esteem of those so afflicted), and so people with this condition were now labeled "physically handicapped". Originally, the term "handicap" described a disadvantage given to a player in a game when competing with a player less skilled. Describing someone who has a physical disability as "handicapped" does not describe the person's condition; it merely puts a different "spin" on it for those not so afflicted.

After being used for several years in this new way, however, the term "handicapped" soon came to have many of the same negative connotations as the words "crippled" and "lame," once again causing prejudice and low-self-esteem to rear their ugly heads. Rather than admit their mistake and move on, the advocates of PC decided to invent a neologism in their effort to combat the prejudice against and the low-self-esteem of those with physical deficiencies: "physically challenged." In the heady days of its beginning, while this neologism was still emotionally neutral and definition-free, the proponents of PC worked hard to bring many other previously-clearly-defined terms under the Big Tent of the term "physically challenged." Thanks to their efforts, someone who is physically challenged could be lame or crippled, but could also be weak, blind, deaf, or have any number of other physical difficulties. Thus, while a few individuals may feel a misplaced sense of accomplishment at the use of the new terminology, not only does the population at large still consider someone who is unable to walk physically deficient, but the words that are used to describe that physical deficiency have been made more vague and harder to understand over time, making communication—and therefore accurate understanding—more difficult to attain.

As pernicious as pomo is, however, this book and the ideas herein would not have been possible without it. Pomo's cynicism and logical criticism applied to the most "intuitive" of concepts, its analysis of meaning and the recognition of the subjectivity of language, and the importance it places on questioning all "structure" along with its refusal to call any given structure "good enough" (i.e. beyond criticism), have laid part of the foundation upon which the edifice of this book has been built. These qualities of pomo have made possible the unveiling of the "structure" of the C-K-H process, and its influence on various areas of 20th Century thought, that this book provides. Also, it is pomo that provides readers some of the objectivity and vocabulary needed to assess the ideas presented in this book. The problem with post-modernism lies not in its recognition and analysis of structure, but in its condemnation of all structure. Post-modernists, instead of using their analysis of structure to help increase our understanding, turn their backs on "understanding" itself and seem to seek deification through deconstruction. While, as Nietzsche said, chaos may indeed be necessary to give birth to a dancing star[62], even a dancing star must have structure to exist, and the difference between the star and the night that surrounds it must be recognized if its dance is to be appreciated. Pomo's renunciation of all structure guarantees its eventual oblivion in meaninglessness, and unless pomo's positive contributions are recognized and cultivated separately, those contributions—along with all individuals and cultures who embrace post-modernism—will vanish into a Nietzschean twilight.

As is probably obvious at this point, this author considers pomo to be overall a very negative development. What makes it ominous is the fact that pomo is the *only* significant movement in 20th Century (and so far, in early 21st Century) philosophy, in the sense that it clearly has an influence on thought and language outside of university philosophy departments and library book-selection. Unless something truly new comes along, historical precedent indicates that the total deconstruction of meaning evident now in pomo will be endemic to all areas of thought in fifty to a hundred years. If that happens, it would mean an actual regression in our collective ability to think and comprehend. Concepts that we fully understand and build on usefully now will be unavailable to our descendants, and no new concepts will take their place. The very *cogito* that Descartes, Kant and Hegel used to define and explore our world is now boomeranging back on us, and it will wipe out what hard-earned understanding we do possess if we let it. It's not enough to write off modern economics and philosophy as "mere" misapplications of the C-K-H process; as long as the C-K-H process is the only tool we use to produce understanding, it appears inevitable that it will be applied to all areas of study, even when and where it demonstrably does not work. To prevent these misapplications of the C-K-H process (and to correct those already perpetrated), we need new tools to explore the areas the C-K-H process has failed to illuminate for us.

Before delineating these new tools, however, we should take a look at why the C-K-H process is so appealing, and reaffirm why—like certain elements of pomo—it is and will remain a useful tool in the construction of human understanding. While doing this, we will also learn to recognize indications of C-K-H overuse. This will help us to quickly realize what is happening when we are confronted with the C-K-H process' limits, and so recognize when it is time for us to find new tools.

A Brief Analysis

The Appeal of the C-K-H Process

Up to this point, many of the limitations and internal contradictions of the C-K-H process have been discussed at length. As stated at the end of the previous section, however, there is no denying the usefulness of the C-K-H process or the substantial contributions it has made to modern thought and life. It becomes apparent upon close study that most of the negative results of the C-K-H process are due to its inapplicability to a given subject of study, rather than to a flaw in the process itself. As an analogy, a protractor is no less useful for measuring angles because it cannot be used to pound a nail; a protractor is simply the wrong tool to use to pound a nail.

The next logical question, of course, is: why do we embrace the C-K-H process to the exclusion of everything else? Why have we been using protractors to pound nails for over a hundred years? There are several reasons, all of which will be presented in this section.

Probably the most important reason why the C-K-H process has become the sole process used for producing understanding is because the human condition predisposes us to accept its validity. Our whole lives seem dominated by physical duality: right and left, male and female, light and dark, hot and cold, etc., all of which have recognizable degrees between the opposites, the recognition and balance (or, if you will, reduction to and synthesis) of which is a necessary goal for the sake of survival, understanding and comfort.

As we turn to the social realm, we encounter a second reason why the C-K-H process is so appealing: it often appears to conveniently simplify complex issues. Examples of this simplification include the concepts of right and wrong, good and bad, "conservative" and "liberal" and (probably the most pernicious) us and them. Whether or not the results provided by these convenient simplifications are satisfactory over the long-term will be addressed in the next section; it is sufficient for now to recognize that most individuals base their perceptions and decisions on these convenient simplifications.

The third reason for the C-K-H process' appeal is the fact it is almost invariably effective in the short-term, providing satisfactory—even excellent—results. Examples of this short-term effectiveness can be found on almost any level (mixing hot and cold water to attain a comfortable water temperature, reacting suspiciously to someone who is not dressed or acting appropriately, identifying someone as "bad" when they are caught telling a lie, etc.). Phenomena that cannot be addressed effectively using the C-K-H process—such as the fact that all physical objects must have three independent dimensions, rather than interdependent ones—are often simply ignored, which the overall short-term effectiveness of the C-K-H process makes easy to do. Since a majority of humanity appears to rarely think beyond the short-term, it's not surprising that something that proves both easy and convenient for producing accurate short-term assessments would be widely adopted.

This basic plausibility of the reduction-and-synthesis presented by the C-K-H process, along with its demonstrable effectiveness when applied to many areas of life, guarantee the C-K-H process' continued use and usability in human affairs. It appears foolish to cast aside a tool that has been so effective in the past, and continues to be so today in many areas. It is fortunate this tool has proven so useful, since for so long it has been the only one available for creating intellectual understanding.

While other world-views existed and continue to exist outside of the C-K-H process (e.g. Aristotelian, shamanistic), their inability to advance understanding past a certain point "given" in nature, or beyond other fundamental "givens," makes them unable to compete with the C-K-H process' seeming ability to "advance" (i.e. increase the understanding available to) indefinitely the understanding of those who use it. This seeming universal applicability for "advancement" has been a stronger encouragement towards adoption and application of the C-K-H process, than any disincentive instinct, custom or contrary education has been able to provide.

Unfortunately for the C-K-H process and its application, as a society we have now passed the limits of its usefulness (its potential to "advance" us), and as a result have been finding our "advancement" halted—or even reversed—while we still believe we are going forward. For example, the idea of "ownership" and its importance in social (and especially financial) affairs is undeniable and ubiquitous. However, because this idea has never been "understood" (i.e. studied, analyzed and effectively defined), only vaguely assumed, it has been subjected to multiple indignities over the past two hundred years, as various thinkers have tried—and failed—to "understand" it with an inappropriate tool (the C-K-H process). Examples of these indignities include Karl Marx's treatment of the idea—that the state is the only rightful owner of property, a situation that has proven antithetical to human nature—and Keynes' treatment of the idea: that borrowing is the same thing as owning. These two ideas are disturbingly similar to each other, and equally inadequate for describing human experience. The mistreatment of the idea of "ownership" by the C-K-H process serves as an example of the myopia and confusion the C-K-H process produces when misapplied. In the next Chapter, "ownership" will be analyzed and effectively defined, as an illustration of how to transcend the C-K-H process.

Some evidence of the C-K-H process' practical limitations—and its simultaneously unlimited appeal—has been presented previously (see the sections on economics, pomo, and the description of the abuses perpetrated upon the idea of ownership enumerated above), and more evidence will be presented in the following two sections.

The Long-Term Problem

The C-K-H process consistently fails to discern the truth when applied to phenomena that span long reaches of space, time, or variation.

As pointed out in the previous section, some things are not containable in opposites. A good example of the C-K-H process' effect on cognition is our use of the term "black and white mentality", denoting a mind-set that only perceives two mutually exclusive extremes in a given situation. The effect of the C-K-H process is not so much apparent in our ability to apprehend the term, however, but in our perception of its "opposition" in the idea that any given issue has "shades of grey," meaning that there are possible syntheses or degrees between the two opposites. While this is often true—or, following our visual metaphor, black, white, and shades of grey certainly do exist and can be usefully attributed to certain phenomena—no significant opposition has been presented; grey, as a synthesis of black and white, does not truly constitute something "different" from black and white, and therefore the "black and white mentality" remains essentially unopposed. An idea would have to both escape the black-grey-white spectrum entirely, and introduce something equally real (e.g. the color orange) in order to truly present a different view, which then could, although it not necessarily would, oppose the original idea.

A real-world example might be useful at this point. In the early 21st Century, an American President—George W. Bush—issued a statement to the world after a spectacular act of terrorism was perpetrated on United States soil, proclaiming that "you are either with us, or with the terrorists." This is a very stark example of a black-and-white, us-versus-them mentality; other nations and organized social groups were put on notice that they either help the United States government hunt down and eliminate terrorists (become "one of us") or be considered a terrorist oneself by the United States federal government, and therefore an enemy (become "one of them"). There certainly are nations that appear to be firmly in the "us" camp—the U.S., Japan, Israel—nations firmly in the "them" camp—Syria, Iran, Sudan—and (as presented by those who mean to present an opposition to the us-and-them mentality made explicit in Bush's speech) many that fall somewhere in between, creating "shades of grey," such as Pakistan, China, and Russia. However, despite the rhetoric from both the Bush administration and those who claimed to "oppose" the sentiment he expressed, there are nations that don't appear to fit into this black-grey-white spectrum at all. For example, it is very unlikely that the nation of North Korea supports the United States' federal government's post-911 policies (with its Communist government, nuclear brinksmanship, and proven counterfeiting of U.S. currency, they are a prime target for a "pre-emptive strike"), but it is equally unlikely that they would support al-Qaeda (the organization responsible for the act of terrorism mentioned earlier), since al-Qaeda's Islamicism would conflict strongly with its own Communist ideology which views all religion as "the opiate of the masses", something to be recognized as a scourge and eliminated. North Korea, with its "red" policies, upsets the "you are with us or you are with the terrorists" (black-grey-white) applecart constructed by the Bush administration's rhetoric.

This observation brings us to the next difficulty with the simplification provided by the C-K-H process: the fact that the C-K-H process blinds us to anything that does not fit into the pre-determined idea of how reality "should" look. The general lack of perspective noted on the "black and white mentality" above, illustrated by the fact that there is no recognition of North Korea's (and other nations') probable hostility to both al-Qaeda and the U.S. federal government, is sufficient example to allow the discussion to move on.

The outgrowth of this willful blindness is the limitation of understanding. As pointed out previously in the areas of economics, current philosophy, and now politics, sole reliance on the C-K-H process is crippling to an individual's or society's ability to perceive and respond to the world, especially in the long-term—so much debt is accrued that it becomes un-payable, deconstructed language becomes meaningless, the United States will probably be blindsided by an economic coup from East Asia in the next decade as it concentrates on the Middle East and its own financial woes. This indicates that sole use of the C-K-H process does not create a sustainable condition for the individual or society, but a kind of intellectual "short-sightedness". Phenomena nearby in space and time appear important and clearly defined (even if they are not), while distant things—and even distance itself—are considered inconsequential.

Three Indications of C-K-H Overuse

In addition to the negative side-effects already discussed, there are three clear indications that the C-K-H process is being overused by an individual or society: an overarching "zero-sum" mentality, an inability to create (explanation taking the place of creation), and when the polarity of opposites is made meaningless by the opposites' equivalence to each other, often making it impossible to create a functional synthesis from them.

First and foremost of these indications is the presence of an overarching zero-sum mentality. This mentality is based on four assumptions:

a.) All relevant facts are known
b.) All resources are finite
c.) There is not enough of any given resource for the needs of all, and therefore
d.) All resources must be allocated, competed for, or otherwise artificially distributed

This mindset can be considered "overarching" when the concept of "enough" (i.e. abundance being made possible through adaptation as well as production) disappears. As with the appeal of the C-K-H process itself, a zero-sum mentality exercises an almost irresistible intellectual and emotional pull on many of us. From the time most of us are infants, we learn that there is only so much time, so much love, so much money that is generally available, and that we need to work, compete for, or be given a share of the general stock or else do without (with the idea of "doing without" being made an object of fear). This phenomenon compliments and reinforces the interplay of opposites—especially as presented by Kant—apparent in the C-K-H process, where all being is a point on a line; motion toward one pole ("winning", for example) automatically and unavoidably moves one away from the opposite pole ("losing"). While we live in a finite world with finite resources, where competition and bipolarity certainly exist, not everything is a zero-sum game. Much of how life has developed—such as its dependence on the availability of sunlight, the food chain, the way plants and animals provide each other breathable air—seems to create and expand an abundance for all, rather than merely competing for resources already available. The fact that a plant uses sunlight to photosynthesize does not deprive the plant next to it of the same height of this sunlight. "Use" in this case is not the same thing as "consumption."

An overarching zero-sum mentality assumes that "use" and "consumption" cannot be separated. While zero-sum situations certainly exist in nature—moisture in a desert, for example—they tend to be the exception rather than the rule. Most sustainable ecosystems are sustainable because they promote growth (or at least stability) for all its component organisms, without allowing one or a few organisms to gain a monopoly on resources. Even if trees monopolize sunlight in a dense-canopy rainforest, the trees use this sunlight to provide oxygen, sustenance, living space, and a basis of the food-chain for the rain-forest's other inhabitants. The trees actively create other utilizable resources, thereby ensuring abundance. If a zero-sum situation occurs in an ecosystem, it is often due to an imbalance. This imbalance then creates a negative feedback loop, limiting itself in time and space to be eventually replaced by a more abundant situation. For example, let us say predators become scarce in a given ecosystem because of a disease that affects them but not their prey. The predator's prey begins to overpopulate the area, and quickly use up the food supply the local ecosystem provides them. *Ceteris paribus*, there are three possibilities for what happens next: The prey die back to a number that the local ecosystem can sustain, the prey adapt to the changing conditions, or the prey move out of the area. All three options restore the ecosystem's equilibrium and allow the resumption of the gradual increase of abundance for all organisms involved.

Humanity is the only organism that produces true "waste." "Waste" is an unknown concept in nature, since the "waste products" (i.e. by-products of digestion, respiration and death) of one organism are sustenance for at least one other organism, and often multiple others. "Waste" and "pollution" as modern man understands these terms (i.e. by-products of consumption totally unusable by any organism or system) are the results of an overarching zero-sum mentality. Trapped in an adolescent competition for resources and unable to perceive the inherent abundance of these resources over time, the finite resources available in the moment are refined for a single use, "consumed," and cast aside in a form totally unusable by humanity or by any other part of any known ecosystem. Instead of zero-sum situations being exceptional (and therefore allowing the need to construct them as a negative feedback loop to be perceived), they are considered the rule, and are constructed as positive feedback loops. This means that the imbalance creates further imbalance, rather than self-correction. An iconic example of these zero-sum situations creating positive feedback loops would be the refinement of petroleum. This process produces a large—but finite—amount of energy in the short-term, which in the forms of plastics and fuel are the basis of modern culture. However, petroleum appears to be a finite resource, and the refined product is good for but a single use. Once used, it cannot be reused or usefully altered, yet its use is so convenient that over time humanity demands ever more of it. This increasing demand becomes ever harder to meet, even as piles of un-reusable plastics and clouds of undesirable fumes become ever more choking.

This insanity is made possible, in part, by total reliance on the C-K-H process to understand the world around us. This dependence blinds individuals and societies to the reality of non-zero-sum situations and to the possibility of creating "non-zero-sum games."

This is not a call to abandon technology as we understand it today. Instead, the point is being made that the way we have applied technology does not sustain our continued existence on this planet. The planet will continue to exist, one way or another, but under certain circumstances it may continue to do so without us.

There are three reasons for this misapplication of science:

1. The inability of a zero-sum-dominated mind to conceive of "enough" (i.e. abundance being made possible through adaptation as well as production)
2. The need to have more than someone else and thereby "win"
3. The inability to create anything new, only explain and refine what is already present

The concept of "enough" has already been defined, and the need to win is fairly self-explanatory. The inability to create, however, is more complex and will be addressed here in detail.

Continuing with the examples of nature and technology, it could be immediately pointed out that humankind in all societies has been the sole creator of technology. The wheel, fire, agriculture, musical instruments, the shaping and use of metal, and clothing are all well-known examples. While technology is apparently an example of creation—new items and processes are created, which in turn make possible other items and processes—as we have practiced it until now, it has really been a process of explanation and refinement of what we find in nature.

For example, pharmaceuticals are created from combinations of different organic compounds, each combination being designed to interact with the human body in a certain way. While the individual compounds may be unknown in nature, they are the result of a process of explanation and refinement of nature, which we call chemistry. In chemistry, known compounds (and in the final analysis, known elements, all provided for by nature) have their various properties defined and explained, and are combined with other compounds to refine the desired effect when interacting with the human body. These interactions, in turn, are based on the definition and explanation of processes within the human body, and the explanation of how different things interact with biological processes in the human body. This is known as the study of medicine. Neither aspirin nor morphine is truly a new creation, merely a refinement of a form already in nature; one comes from birch-bark, the other from the flower of the poppy plant. Both, when ingested in their natural or refined form, interact with and alter the physiology of the human body, but neither creates anything new in the body that the body's system as a whole can use. These substances merely manipulate the resources and processes already present in the body to create a short-term effect.

Generally, the only long-term upshot of these manipulations is to disrupt the processes being manipulated (a form of reduction). This limits the long-term usability of this technology. The long-term use of aspirin can create ulcers in the stomach, while morphine use can lead to morphine addiction. Not only can there never be "enough" in terms of production, but the adaptations that follow from the extended use of this technology (i.e. injury and addiction) actively reduce the health—the overall functionality and viability—of the individual.

This is but one example. The process just described in the creation of technology and its eventual results—definition, explanation, synthesis, reduction—is endemic. One would think that after a couple of experiences with short-term solutions followed by long-term failure or disastrous side-effects, a rational individual or society would seek sustainable, long-term solutions. Instead, the same failed technological model is applied over and over again, producing the same results of short-term success and long-term failure. Instead of pharmaceutical developers changing their focus to understanding the causes of affliction in the human body, encouraging the elimination of underlying causes and thereby increasing the overall "health" of the individual (perhaps supplemented by short-term application of pain- or other symptom-suppressants), their energies are still focused on developing "better" (i.e. more effective in the short-term) pain- or symptom-suppressants. While this approach to technology is useful in the short-term, it is detrimental in the long-term. In this, it has a great similarity to the C-K-H process, and is an elegant illustration of the relation between the two intellectual approaches.

The solution to this seeming impasse is not to abandon technology as it has developed, but to augment its process of definition-explanation-synthesis-reduction with the process of creation, and an emphasis on balance rather than manipulation. There currently are cultural movements in the early 21st Century United States that encourage the balance-over-manipulation model of technology—such as the permaculture movement and holistic medicine—and even some examples of technology based on this model (such as wind and solar power generation, and homeopathy). However, a general cultural imperative to integrate and advance this model, and to create instead of just explain, appears to still be lacking. The current state of technology threatens human welfare over the long-term. The insanity is that even when confronted with this fact, our intellectual "short-sightedness" assures us that this something we can safely leave to our children to deal with.

And finally, there is the problem of the perceived equivalence of opposites. While this has been often pointed out as a problem in the political sphere—such as in George Orwell's classic novel "Animal Farm," a parable of political revolt where the leaders of a successful barnyard revolution come to exactly resemble the murderous tyrants they deposed—the advent of post-modern discourse has brought the problem forward in other areas. An excellent example of this already discussed is Keynesian economics, which takes the three potential uses of capital—saving, investment, and consumption—and redefines them as various methods of consumption, making all three equivalent, and the use of capital in "consumption" the first among equals.[1] Although this attractive idea has sadly proven to be a false synthesis, the continuing belief in this idea still causes no end of mischief. This idea of the unity of capital-use is perfectly consistent logically, perfectly acceptable intellectually, and quite common and convenient socially. The appeal and continued use of this false idea (and the difficulties that arise from its use) will likely continue as long as the underlying idea of the equivalence of opposites is entrenched in the culture.

It is probably apparent by this point that most individuals—and societies—in the world exhibit symptoms of overuse of the C-K-H process. The next chapter will discuss alternatives to the C-K-H process for producing understanding, and demonstrate possible areas of application for these alternatives.

What Could Happen?

What will happen if the C-K-H process continues to be misapplied? As quantum mechanics teaches us, while no one has yet found a foolproof way of predicting the future, there is always a range of possible outcomes, some of which are more probable than others. The least probable (but still technically possible) outcome in this instance is that nothing will change. History teaches us that change is the only constant in human affairs, if not in human motivation, so this possibility can be confidently discounted. The second least probable outcome is that of positive or "new" knowledge increasing and our overall situation changing for the better. Welcome innovations in physics, medicine, and the new science of psychology developed over the course of the 20th Century should have increased our general well-being, but have failed to do so. Our comfort and longevity have increased, but mis-education and self-destructive behavior has increased in lockstep, negating much of the benefit we would otherwise have seen to our general well-being. The significant tangible creations of 20th Century physics—nuclear fission arguably being its pinnacle—have been deadlier explosives and deadlier wastes than the planet's biosphere can deal with. Psychology, while a useful tool for those few willing and able to take the arduous path of self-discovery, has been applied with greatest impact in the areas of politics and marketing. This has led to the manipulation of the masses into buying products or supporting policies that are harmful to all but a few, and has helped make these manipulations appear to be the inevitable price of progress. As has been shown in previous chapters, misapplication of the C-K-H process has already wreaked havoc in the areas of economics, philosophy, politics, and language, actively reducing understanding and the ability to reason effectively; this is the opposite of gaining new knowledge, and since this appears to be the current trend, gaining new knowledge in the future (and making positive changes) appears improbable without first acquiring new tools of understanding that would allow us to reverse the current trend. This brings us to a third possibility, unfortunately the most probable of those listed here (especially since it is already visible as a trend) unless new tools for producing understanding are acquired: the

69

continuing decrease of accurate and useful understanding, accompanied by the expansion of self-destructive behavior. The "new thing" in philosophy, at the beginning of the 21st Century, is something called "intellectual conservatism" or "essentialism" (a philosophical movement newer than post-modernism, still too new to make itself felt outside the field of philosophy) which, in reaction to post-modernism, is leading a self-confessed retreat to the knowledge-taken-on-faith of Augustine, Thomas Aquinas, and Plato. This is advertised as a way to "oppose" post-modernist thought[1]. Not only is this movement patently derivative from start to finish, but the philosophies espoused were successfully supplanted by the Cartesian approach to understanding (and therefore its defeat by the C-K-H process seems a foregone conclusion, since the C-K-H process is arguably a refinement of Descartes' success) three hundred and fifty years ago. It seems as if this "essentialism" is an act of desperation, perpetrated by a few who recognize that a way out of post-modernism is needed, but cannot find one, and so figuratively bury their heads in the sand. As pointed out previously in this book, since at least the Renaissance the study of philosophy has been a bellwether for all other areas of study; where philosophy goes, all other studies eventually follow. The field of philosophy's current two-fold rejection of discovery in understanding—through deconstruction in post-modernism, and the demand for the return of "received truth" in essentialism—does not bode well for the future advancement of understanding. As has been observable since the Renaissance, it is only when new discoveries in understanding are attained through philosophy that advancement in other fields of study follows. Current philosophy's rejection of understanding makes the active erasure and limitation of understanding in the future much more probable than any other possibility, at this point.

How far could this potential destruction of understanding proceed? Once again, it's hard to say with any certainty. What does seem certain, based on the analysis presented here, is that without a process for attaining understanding other than the Cartesian-Kantian-Hegelian one, the best that can be hoped for in any area of study is a delaying action, preserving ideas handed down in a kind of suspended animation like family heirlooms, used to define forevermore our cultural identity. This suspended animation of ideas, the very tactic proposed by essentialism, was exactly the state of affairs that prevented advancement in understanding in medieval Europe, and was what Cartesian thought supplanted. Clearly, there is no final victory for understanding possible in employing this stratagem. Therefore, we need new tools to attain discoveries in understanding, to make advancement and improvement possible, or risk continued degeneration. Using a biblical metaphor earlier to describe the positions of Descartes', Kant's and Hegel's philosophies in the modern world was a deliberate choice. The C-K-H process has become *the* God that dictates how we understand our world. As Jung stated in the quote that begins this book, this "attempt to make one out of the many" (i.e. the attempt to understand all phenomena using a single thought process) has "created the torment of incomprehension, and the mutilation of the created world, the essence and law of which is diversity." New tools for understanding—new Gods—must be brought forth that can equal the power of the C-K-H process, if we are to undo the damage already done and increase our understanding and well-being, if we are to heal our self-mutilation. Presenting a potential new tool for the discovery of understanding, and thereby providing some hope for our collective future, is the purpose of this book.

The New Tool

First, it is necessary to acknowledge the fact that while some phenomena are truly understandable as interplays of opposites, others simply are not, and those that are not cannot be understood through the C-K-H process. Phenomena whose behavior cannot be reliably predicted by reduction-and-synthesis probably lie outside the purview of the C-K-H process, and must be analyzed in a non-dualistic way if understanding is to be attained. Thinking based on reduction-and-synthesis must be recognized and suspended, in order to properly apprehend non-dualistic phenomena in their totality. While application of the C-K-H process may produce a partial understanding of non-dualistic phenomena, this understanding can never be made complete until all axes of meaning—all "dimensions" that make up our experience of a given phenomenon—are recognized and taken into account. Some—even many—phenomena can be completely understood by applying the C-K-H process, but as demonstrated earlier, there are others that cannot be.

I often find it useful to use the idea of three dimensions as a beginning when analyzing any phenomenon, whether apparently dualistic or not, I come across. The search for a third axis this beginning entails often serves as a good starting place, yet it can be a mistake to assume there should be three axes of meaning to any given phenomena. One of the examples presented below of non-dualistic phenomena has four axes of meaning, and in some cases (such as color vision versus vision only incorporating shades of light and dark) the number of axes is much higher. As stated above, there are also some phenomena that are truly dualistic, and it's important not to invent axes of meaning where none are. Phenomena with only a single axis of meaning are at least a theoretical possibility, although no examples spring immediately to mind. Nevertheless, ruling out the existence of mono-axial phenomena is probably a mistake.

An axis of meaning is a factor that defines the experience a given phenomenon whenever and however it manifests, and movement along this axis (an increase or decrease in the presence of this factor) corresponds to a change in the experience of the phenomena it describes in a consistent, significant way.

When a phenomenon's features are described in their totality, and its behavior is consistently and accurately predicted *a posteriori*, then it can be said that understanding of that phenomenon has been attained.

Examples of phenomena that cannot be completely understood when reduced to interplays of opposites will be given below, along with their axes of meaning. New analyses of these phenomena that— to the best of this author's knowledge and ability—are divorced from the C-K-H process will also be presented. It is sincerely hoped that these examples will inspire others not merely to follow up and build on the examples given, but to encourage the recognition of other non-dualistic phenomena, thereby further expanding our possible realm of understanding.

Five examples of apparently non-dualistic phenomena will be presented below, each one in a different area of human understanding and study: First, an example in how we experience the physical world. Second and third, in the area of economics, a new analysis will be given of the theory of value, and an important factor in market exchange will be examined. Fourth, in the area of psychology, Freud's analysis of the nature and interplay of the sex-drive/death-wish duality will be re-examined. And finally, in the area of philosophy, the relationship of cause and effect will be re-examined.

We will begin our three-dimensional explorations with a look at our experience of the "third dimension" itself.

Two-Dimensional Thinking In A Three Dimensional World

In previous chapters, the history of the C-K-H process has been outlined, along with why it has been and continues to be so appealing. One of the key features of the C-K-H process (as first outlined by Kant, and expanded upon by Hegel) is the reduction of all phenomena to an essential duality. This section will be the first of five sections presenting phenomena that are not reducible to an essential duality, and illustrating how treating them as so reducible has prevented complete understanding in these areas. And also, how looking at these non-dualistic phenomena as they are broadens our understanding and our ability to adapt to the world as we find it.

Hegel demonstrated in his book Science of Logic that all forms of measure consist of a duality, in the form of a ratio between an object (the thing being measured) and everything else. This ratio describes a boundary between the object measured and the rest of the world[2]. For example, a standard 8 ½" x 11" sheet of paper has 11" of itself along two of its sides and 8" of itself along the other two (along with however many micrometers of depth). Each end of each side is described by the ending of the sheet of paper and the beginning of something else, such as empty air, a desk, or another sheet of paper. This ratio of thing-being-measured to thing-not-being-measured is what gives us measure...in this case, 8 ½" of width, 11" of length, and however many micrometers of depth. Also, using Hegel's definition of measure (which, consciously or not, is the definition most of us use) a given object can be generally described as "larger" or "smaller" relative to another object. For instance, an 8 ½" x 11" sheet of paper is "smaller" that an 11" x 14" piece of paper, in length, width and total area. This process produces clear, consistent understanding of phenomena, and therefore has proven useful.

However, this process of "measurement" and the understanding it produces is limited, since it fails to fully account for an object's physical existence. Two essential facts of physical existence remain unaccounted for, specifically that:

#1: All physical objects are three-dimensional
#2: The three dimensions—height, width, and depth—all necessitate each other in an object, but do not automatically add or subtract from each other as a function of their existence.

No element of the C-K-H process can account for the fact that an object must have three necessary but independent dimensions—three axes of meaning—in order to exist physically. While two-dimensional and single-dimensional *representations* of phenomena are certainly possible and even useful in describing—or "measuring"—very discrete *parts* of our three-dimensional world, a dualistic representation (the only kind possible when using the C-K-H process) of any physical totality will always be incomplete, because it lacks the scope to describe the actual three-dimensional reality in which we live. This brings us directly to the second fact listed above, also unacknowledged by the C-K-H process: that while all three dimensions are necessary (no physical object can exist without all three dimensions), they are also *independent of each other*. While there certainly is an observable ratio between each of any object's three physical dimensions, no ratio between the three dimensions can be said to hold true for all objects at all times. These dimensions cannot be reduced to pairs of opposites relative to each other in any consistent way, which means that they cannot be reduced to an underlying unity, either. To continue with the example used above of sheets of paper, just because a sheet of paper measures 11" on one side, does not necessitate a particular measure—or even a particular ratio of measure—of a side perpendicular to it. While we currently have standardized paper sizes (e.g. 8 ½ x 11, 11 x 14, etc.) and paper-thickness, there is no physical law dictating these proportions; they are a matter of convention only.

If the C-K-H process truly described the world, then length, width, and depth—assuming that all three could exist in a single object—as interplays of opposites, would all define each other through observable ratios in all physical objects. This would mean that altering the measure of something's length would automatically alter one or both of the other dimensions in a consistent way. This is not how things work in the physical world we inhabit. If one takes an 11 x 14 inch piece of paper and cuts 3" off its length, its total area is reduced but its width and depth remain unchanged. If the C-K-H process consistently applied to physical proportions, this should not be possible; width and/or depth being an opposite of length, width and/or depth would have to maintain a consistent ratio with length as a function of their underlying unity, or else be disassociated with the object described. Even accepting that opposites are equivalent, as interplays of opposites that define a whole, a decrease in one dimension would necessitate a change in any other dimensions that describe a given object.

As has already been shown—and as should be evident from experience—the C-K-H process does not and cannot describe most physical objects. While there are examples of objects where the C-K-H process' requirement for fixed-proportion does hold true—any instance when an object's shape changes but its total area remains the same, such as when a piece of clay is molded—experience says there is no physical law dictating that all objects keep fixed proportions between the dimensions that describe them. Objects that maintain a uniform total area are the exception, not the rule. Most such exceptional objects are artificial, whether by construction or definition.

If our minds always expect to perceive artificial objects—that minority of phenomena whose dimensions are dualistically interdependent—as dictated by the C-K-H process, rather than the kind that most often occur in nature (ones with three independent physical dimensions), it's not so surprising that "real life" comes as such a shock to so many of us. The dualistic way we "measure"—and so attempt to understand—physical objects colors our understanding (or how we "take the measure") of situations and other phenomena that are less grossly physical. We are inclined to think of interdependent dualities—action and reaction, give and take, beginning and end—when we interact with our world, rather than looking for and finding all the independent dimensions that compose an experience or an interaction. And so when phenomena reveal dimensions beyond the two that we expect of them—when the action we take does not cause the expected reaction, when we give to others but are not allowed to take from them as we expect, or when the day that begins according to plan does not end that way—we are more often fearful, angry, and baffled than observant, curious, and adaptable. We are inclined to salve our discomfort with the belief that we have been wronged or misunderstood, rather than seeking out, acknowledging, and correcting the deficiencies of our own expectations or perceptions. The situations that we do encounter which conform to our interdependently dualistic expectations merely reinforce a kind of myopia. This myopia, while granting us some immediate comfort when things do not go as we expect, limits both our perceptions and our ability to adapt to things as they are. This self-imposed defect limits our ability to understand our circumstances, and ultimately our ability to survive and prosper both individually and collectively.

Although the fact that most physical objects have three independent—rather than interdependent—dimensions is something most of us would say we were already aware, very few of us ever pause and reason through the implications of this fact. This gross physical exception to interdependent duality impacts us every second of our lives, yet despite its constant presence we somehow still expect that every experience can be—or should be—intellectually understandable through interdependent dualism. Due to the interdependently dualistic way that we measure—necessitated by our misapplication of the C-K-H process to produce understanding—we have blinded ourselves to the limitations this use of two-dimensional forms of measurement have placed on our comprehension of our three-dimensional world. If we have been effectively blind to something so ubiquitous, what else might we have not seen?

The Four Dimensions of Value

"Value" is a multi-faceted and highly subjective word. In this text, it will be defined and discussed as an economic term. Specifically, "value," in this text, will be defined as the wealth provided by a good or service.

Even in the narrow economic sense, however, many economists disagree as to how to determine a thing's value. The most commonly accepted way to define a thing's value in today's economic circles, is as a combination of the item's utility (i.e. usefulness) and its scarcity (i.e. how difficult it is to acquire). While other methods of determining a thing's value exist (such as value being a relationship between a thing's utility and exchangeability[3]), all economic methods of discovering value have a dualistic base. Value is always calculated by economists through discovering the relationship between two distinct variables. The third and fourth "dimensions" about to be discussed apply to all known economic methods of discovering value.

The "third dimension" of value may best be described as "popularity." This is a description of how desirable a thing is at a given time, whether for rational reasons (shovels during snow season) or irrational reasons (most women's fashions). Clothing, music, neighborhoods, contact information, stock certificates, and most other traded goods are all affected by how popular they are at a given time. The more popular something is, the greater its perceived value will be. Popularity is probably the most fluid of value's axes of meaning, being often the least tied to any objective considerations. Popularity is an artifact of conscious consensus; whatever the group of buyers of a particular good or service decide is desirable, will be imbued with popularity. A popular item is likely to rise in price even as its quantity increases, or as the market is faced with other factors that would normally drive down the item's price, such as declining quality. Popularity can also allow goods to be more easily traded than other less popular goods of similar quantity in a similarly capitalized market. It is vitally important to take popularity into account when determining the value of any kind of short-term transaction, and usually for the timing of a longer-term transaction as well (when to sell something bought for investment purposes, for example).

Popularity is an example of consensus creating truth, where the opinions and subjective experience of a majority have a significant impact on objective reality.

The "fourth dimension" of value is, very simply, the concept of "ownership." "Ownership" is not simply the use of a thing, or having one's name on a piece of paper that says one "owns" it. "Ownership," as defined here, means *having final (and preferably absolute) say over the use and disposal of a given good or service.* Having "ownership" of a thing (or "owning" it) makes it considerably more "valuable" (i.e. imbued with value) to its "owner" (i.e. the one who has ownership of it). Not only does the owner have access to the entire material security (i.e. "wealth") provided by the good or service, but the person's "ownership" of other assets is not put in jeopardy in order to maintain this security. A person's overall "ownership" of assets (and by extension, their "wealth") is put at risk, the more a person's capital is invested in the use of things that the person does not "own."

Here is an example of how ownership affects the overall wealth of an individual. Bob and Jane have both purchased used sports cars of the same make, model and year, for the same sticker price: $24,000. Bob paid the $24,000 up front, in full. He can be said to truly "own" the car. Bob now has no obligation to the car dealer or any lender regarding the use and disposal of this vehicle, and as long as Bob pays any registration fee due to the state he resides in and follows all applicable laws, the state will probably have very little to say regarding how he uses or disposes of it. Bob can do what he wants with his car, take care of it (or not) as he sees fit, and any money he may make in the use or disposal of the car—including selling it—goes directly to him. Also, Bob will not have to pay one cent more to retain use of the car than maintenance and his own tastes call for.

Because Bob has ownership of the car, he is able to take full advantage of the car's utility (its usefulness to him personally) and its scarcity (resale or social value), minus costs for maintenance, upkeep, insurance, and any other expenses Bob decides the vehicle requires (most of which Bob will have a fair degree of flexibility in when deciding when, if, and how to pay them). Bob has the maximum possible access to the material security—the "wealth"—provided by the car, because he owns it.

On the other hand, our other buyer, Jane, put down a $6,000 down payment on the car, borrowed the other $18,000 of the list price at 5% interest, and has worked out a three year payment plan with the bank that lent her the money. Although the title of the vehicle may very well be in Jane's name, she does not really own it. After driving the car off the dealer's lot, she will still have extraordinary obligations to the bank that lent her money, regarding the car she now supposedly owns. These obligations, if not discharged properly, will cost her the use of the car. The proper discharge of these obligations puts a significant amount of her other wealth at risk.

In addition to paying the bank the $18,000 it originally loaned her, the loan was made at 5% interest compounded annually. This means Jane will owe an additional $2700 (15% of the original loan). For car loans in the U.S., the interest is often demanded up-front by the bank after the loan is issued, to make sure that they do not lose any potential earnings if the loan is paid off early. Banks also often demand the "owner" of a car partially bought by the bank purchase full-coverage insurance on the automobile, costing Jane quite a bit more than would otherwise be required. The bank has no obligation to defray costs or otherwise absorb the risk involved with Jane's use of the car, such as insurance or maintenance; all such expenses (including those associated with theft or the destruction of the car) are Jane's responsibility, and do not in any way reduce the amount she owes to the bank. If Jane decides to sell the car herself before her loan is repaid, any money she gets from the sale of the car—up to the amount of her remaining debt—goes to the bank instead of her. If the sale of the car does not cover her remaining debt, she is still responsible for paying back the balance of the loan.

Two facts are starkly evident in this example: first, that the bank is the real "owner" of the car until Jane pays off her loan. Even though Jane's name is on the title, she only has use of her car at the whim of the bank, and so cannot be said to "own" it as that term is understood here; she owns the car in name, and is allowed use of it, but does not "own" it in fact. Secondly, Jane pays a lot more for the privilege of driving her car than Bob does. Interest, higher insurance payments, the inability to make use of the full resale value of the car, and the inability to walk away from it if necessary; all these things make Jane's experience of her car a much more expensive one than

Bob's, putting a lot more of what other wealth she may possess at risk.

As stated at the end of the short paragraph on popularity, popularity is an example of consensus creating truth. Ownership's axis of meaning to value is an example of a very different—but equally important—phenomenon, which is that of truth transcending consensus. Truth transcending consensus is in some ways the opposite of consensus creating truth. Ownership is an artifact of conditions we have no control over (either because these conditions are bigger than we are or because we are not conscious of participating in them), instead of conscious consensus. While ownership may have a relatively limited role in ascertaining the value of short-term transactions, it is a vital factor in determining the value of any long-term one. This is the opposite of popularity's interaction with value. When truth transcends consensus (as it does with ownership), objective circumstances shape subjective experiences; this is the opposite of popularity, where subjective perceptions shape objective circumstances. It is a mistake to take this analysis of opposites too far, however; popularity and ownership—as well as other examples of consensus creating truth and truth transcending consensus—can co-exist, even if they often don't. Sometimes a long-term truth is immensely popular, and sometimes owning the right thing at a time when it is unpopular can plunge one into poverty.

To repeat, "value" as defined here is the wealth (i.e. material security) provided by a good or service. Both popularity and ownership of a good or service must be taken into consideration when calculating a thing's economic value, if an undistorted perception of economic value—and wealth—is to be acquired. One of the primary reasons lasting wealth is so difficult for so many people to gain is because most people do not have a clear understanding of economic value. When viewing a thing's value as the intersection of scarcity, utility, popularity, and ownership (and given the discipline and freedom to apply these principles properly), it is much easier to recognize value—or its absence—and so wisely acquire or avoid those things that would change the status of one's wealth. Even if an individual has no desire to "get rich," the financial stability created by viewing value in this way gives any individual much greater personal freedom and potential adaptability. This freedom and adaptability is not available to someone with a limited, or typically two-dimensional, perception of value.

Brokering the Market

Most people who bother to think about such things believe that every participant in a market is buyer or a seller, a producer or a consumer, and that every participant in a market is both buyer and seller at different times. This belief is incorrect, and is very likely the reason why so many find market behavior to be irrational and unpredictable. Even in a small local market where everyone exchanges directly with everyone else, this dualistic categorization does not effectively encompass all market participants. Therefore, it cannot effectively describe all market activity, despite its popularity and elegant simplicity.

There are two indispensible classes of participants in markets that cannot be accurately described as either buyers or sellers: brokers of goods and services, and brokers of information. In small markets where most exchange is direct, these intermediaries are present but occupy only a very small niche, allowing them to be easily overlooked (although their influence can be felt strongly under certain conditions). However, as markets become larger and more complex, as "supply chains" become longer, and as exchange becomes increasingly indirect, the influence of these intermediaries grows and the effect of their actions becomes more obvious. When insisting that all market participants must be classed as either buyers or sellers, however, the true nature and activities of intermediaries in a market will always remain misunderstood, no matter how powerful these brokers become or how egregious their influence. The presence of these intermediaries render a dualistic description of market actors incomplete, since a portion of actors in any market—large or small— cannot be appropriately described by the dualistic model of either buyers or sellers, producers or consumers. Since we often try to understand the inherently non-dualistic flow of goods and services within a market using a belief shaped by the dualism inherent in reduction-and-synthesis, it's not surprising that market behavior often surprises and confounds us. When the flow of goods and services that compose a market is looked on as a dynamic phenomenon with four independent axes of meaning rather than an interdependent two, market behavior becomes easier to understand, to trace, and to predict.

Examples of brokers of goods and services include wholesalers of all kinds, the retail industry, the entertainment industry, stock-brokers, and companies that provide temporary employees to other companies. These intermediaries acquire products and services from producers that the intermediaries hope will appeal to potential buyers, and then present these stocks for sale or lease to potential buyers who show an interest. Brokers of information, on the other hand, are those who decide the content and form of information that flows from one group of market actors to another. Examples of information brokers include most educators, all journalists, lawyers, stock-brokers, the publishing industry, and the advertising industry. These intermediaries obtain information that may be of use or interest to certain market actors, and then try to present this information to the appropriate market actors in as attractive a way as possible. While at first glance it would seem that a company or other market actor that acts as one kind of intermediary would logically try to act as the other as well, this dual role is actually the exception rather than the rule (stock-brokers and the entertainment industry being the primary exceptions), which is why the intermediaries discussed here are separated into two different axes of meaning relative to markets, rather than being combined into a single axis.

It's also important not to confuse some forms of producers with these intermediaries. A telecommunications company, for example, is not usually a true broker of goods, services, or information, but is instead the producer of a service. Usually, a telecommunications company is simply providing a service— telecommunication—rather than deciding what information is transmitted or how information is presented. Unless a telecommunications company is censoring, promoting, or otherwise controlling the information transmitted, it is a producer of a service (i.e. telecommunication) rather than a broker of information. As another example, a researcher in any field that communicates the results of his or her original research—such as a college professor when teaching his or her own findings—is not an information broker, but a producer of information. Publishing houses and teaching institutions are part of the information broker axis of any market, and so when the researcher's material is presented through classroom lecture or publication, the information broker axis then typically comes into play. The researcher, however, is still a part of the producer axis, not the information broker axis, in the market of information. Only when a teacher or other educator transmits unoriginal information (i.e. facts or ideas discovered or developed by someone else) do they personally become a broker of information rather than a producer.

Brokers are the "medium" through which the "messages" (goods, services, and information) that compose a market are most often transmitted through. Goods, services, and information that are easily brokered are made much more readily available than they otherwise would be. In contrast, goods, services, and information that are not easily brokered will have difficulty circulating in a market, and it will be more difficult to both buy and sell them conveniently. While it is usually still possible to trade in goods, services, and information not favored by brokers, this trade will often prove costly and inefficient relative to that made possible by intermediaries.

Ideally, the intermediaries in any market have the best interests of both buyers and sellers, producers and consumers, at heart, and so work hard to maximize the welfare of these other groups. In practice, these intermediaries usually have their own interests separate from—and often incompatible with—those of both the buyers and the sellers. This is a key reason why intermediaries compose their own axes of meaning in any given market.

Intermediaries, whether of goods/services or information, are often the least visible (and so least accountable) actors in any market. Because of this, their actions often have the potential to create the greatest and longest-lasting distortions in any market. Classing intermediaries as distinct axes of meaning within a given market, rather than as sub-species of buyers and sellers, helps make their activities more visible and more comprehensible, reducing the possibility of their activities distorting the market in which they participate.

The behavior of intermediaries in a market appears to be very closely tied to the popularity axis of value. In some cases buyers and/or sellers determine what is popular, and this popularity is then catered to by the intermediaries. In other cases, the intermediaries themselves create (or reduce) popularity for a particular good, service, or information. Both the creation and reduction of popularity is effected by the intermediaries by ensuring that only a very limited range of options regarding goods, services, or information is available to certain market actors. This allows the intermediaries to effectively anticipate how these other market actors will behave. By ensuring that they always have a large stock of certain goods available and not others (and/or by presenting information that creates beliefs and expectations regarding the desirability of certain goods), intermediaries can strongly influence the popularity of a good or service. By preventing goods, services or information from circulating in the market, intermediaries can reduce the popularity of goods, services, or information, even in the face of other factors that would otherwise maintain a good's popularity.

In the absence of popularity, there is usually very little broker activity; in developed markets, it is usually in areas that lack popularity where the practice of direct exchange continues to thrive. The used-car market in the United States is an excellent example of this. While there are "used-car dealers" (i.e. brokers of automotive goods) that deal partially or specifically in used automobiles, there is also a substantial trade directly between individuals of same. While the automotive market is big business in the U.S., the direct-exchange-based used car market is significantly smaller, less popular, and less profitable than the market for new cars. Because of this, the used car market is not fully intermediated, and so the options available for both buyers and sellers are often far fewer and of lower-quality than in the new car market.

Buyers, sellers, goods/services brokers, and information brokers are all vital parts of a functioning market. If a market completely lacks any one of these axes of meaning, it will cease to exist. However, certain classes of market actors—certain axes of meaning in the experience of a particular market—will be more powerful at different times. When unemployment is high in an area, potential employers, as buyers of the services of their employees, have more influence in setting the wages (i.e. the price for their employees' service) they pay to those hired in that area. In this case, the buyers in the employment market have the upper hand. If everyone wants to buy a house, those who have a house to sell can ask for a higher price than they might otherwise. This puts the sellers at an advantage in that housing market. In a population where many have lost the knack of entertaining themselves or connecting with others, those intermediaries who bring movies, television shows, games, news, music, apps, and dating prospects to consumers' televisions, computers, iPods, and smart-phones can command a very high price for the privilege of entertaining, informing, or "networking" their target audience. These brokers of entertainment goods are at an advantage over both those who originally produce the entertaining or informational content, and those who wish to buy it, in this kind of a market. If a majority of the population decides that saving for retirement isn't enough, and that they must put their savings directly into stocks and stock-based derivatives in order to come out ahead, then stock-brokers (the information brokers who largely decide who learns what when about different publicly-traded stocks, and how much of any particular stock is available for purchase) can set the price for any stock or stock-based derivative almost exactly as they see fit. This allows the stock-brokers, as brokers of information, a huge amount of control over every part of the stock market.

Markets are artificial structures, although so large and complex they are not usually subject to complete control by a particular actor within or without the market. As artificial structures, they do sometimes operate as zero-sum games, in that the empowering of one axis of meaning's market actors can occur at the expense of those of other axes, without automatically creating a mechanism to correct this imbalance. In nature, when imbalances like this occur they are usually self-correcting; the preponderance of one species in a geographic area makes the situation untenable for other species in the area (including the one that is overabundant), and a new equilibrium is soon found, even if this new equilibrium comes at the expense of one or more species. This is not always the case with markets; sometimes imbalances in markets do correct themselves, but in other cases they become self-perpetuating instead. When self-perpetuating, these imbalances can end up permanently impairing the markets they occur in. The gradual degeneration of worldwide currency markets over the course of the 20th and beginning of the 21st Centuries is an excellent example of this. As the currency markets also illustrate, government regulation or other forms of outside control are not always sufficient to correct these imbalances.

As may already be apparent, markets usually function best—delivering the highest quality and quantity of goods and services the most accurately and quickly at a satisfactory price for all market actors—when all four axes of meaning in a market are more or less equal (i.e. have about the same amount of capital relative to each other, have access to the same relevant information at the same time, and divide the population of market actors roughly equally). It might be appropriate to describe this situation as the "symmetrical market." If this term is deemed appropriate, it would also probably be appropriate to label a market with a sustained, exaggeratedly unequal distribution of capital, information, or population between its axes an "asymmetrical market." The symmetrical market is more likely to be efficient (providing the best and most goods and services at the most satisfactory price for the largest number of participants) than an asymmetrical market, and so in most cases the symmetrical market will be where participation will be best rewarded most consistently. Although it is possible to participate profitably in an asymmetrical market, such as by being a seller in a seller's market, such participation is much riskier than participation in the symmetrical market. Generally, the more briefly one participates in an asymmetrical market, the better off one is.

In markets, capital provides power, to which knowledge provides direction. In an asymmetrical market, outside referees (such as governments or an accrediting body) cannot effectively correct imbalances, in part because the role played by the two different kinds of intermediaries is ignored or underestimated, in part because markets simply move too quickly to be overseen effectively in any kind of bureaucratic fashion, and in part because if a market is regulated, the regulators become yet another axis of meaning within that market, with their own interests and tendencies that can pull the market out of symmetry. The power wielded by those charged with market oversight cannot be informed enough to address the asymmetries in any market (assuming that these overseers are actually interested in doing so), especially if these asymmetries are rooted in the axis composed of either kind of intermediary. Only market actors that cannot be divorced from the market—buyers, sellers, and the two kinds of brokers—can effectively address these asymmetries when they appear. This can be done by individual market actors who, recognizing which axis in a market has a preponderance of assets relative to the other axes (too much capital, too much proprietary information, or too many people), or which axis has too little, choose to circulate their capital away from where it is overabundant, and toward where it is too scarce. If one or a small group of sellers are able to dictate price in a market, it's time for smaller buyers and intermediaries to find other sellers, or other markets to participate in. If buyers can set a market price that's ruinous to the producers of a good, service, or specific kind of information, then it's time for the intermediaries to ensure supplies are reduced, and for producers to find other markets to participate in (possibly with the help of intermediaries). If a market lacks direct exchange outside of its largest buyers and sellers, then one or both kinds of brokers have taken control of that market, and it's time for both buyers and sellers in that market to return to local production and direct exchange, or find other markets to participate in.

As may be apparent, although symmetrical markets probably work better than asymmetrical ones, asymmetrical markets are by far more common. It's possible that the reason for this seemingly irrational situation is the fact that market actors do not understand the nature of their own or others' participation in a given market. With the proper understanding of all axes of meaning in a given market, and what to do when a market is or becomes asymmetrical, it's more likely markets will become easier places to do business in.

If enough market actors choose to circulate their capital intelligently, moving it away from those axes with an overabundance of capital and towards those with a shortage, asymmetries will tend to become symmetries. If market actors choose not to circulate their capital intelligently, asymmetries may very well remain in a given market until and unless the market collapses.

The Psyche's Three Wishes

In his book "The Ego and the Id," Sigmund Freud defined what he called "The Two Classes of Instincts"[4]. These two "classes" of instinct, generally known as the sex-drive and the death-wish, were to become defining features of Freudian psychology's understanding of the human psyche.

According to Freud, the sex drive is "not merely the uninhibited sexual instinct proper...but also the self-preservative instinct" which "aims at complicating life and at the same time, of course, at preserving it"[5]. The death-wish is given the tasks of "leading organic life back to an inorganic state" and "endeavoring to re-establish the state of things that was disturbed by the emergence of life"[6]. This psychic duality propounded by Freud, and the various syntheses derived from it which Freud used to explain human behavior, is a prominent example of the C-K-H process in 20th Century thought. While this duality has been quite useful in explaining some of human motivation, the understanding it has brought has been incomplete. This can be seen in its failure to act as a useful tool in advancing the mental "health" (i.e. functionality and viability) of individuals and society in general. A reason for these failures will be discussed below.

Freud's major error in this area appears to be his fixation on duality. As is obvious from the paraphrase of Freud above, the sex-drive as described by Freud includes not one basic drive, but two: the sex-drive (the individual's wish to procreate), and the will to live (the wish for ego- and biological-survival). The combination of these two drives is then pitted against the death-wish (the wish for ego-death[7]), when only one of these compulsions contained in the sex-drive actually opposes the death-wish. Freud himself recognized that the actual procreative urge is often complicit with the death-wish[8]. In "The Ego and the Id," Freud explains the ego's will to survive as its appropriation of "desexualized libido" from the id (the part of the unconscious mind ruled by instinct rather than reason), which allows the ego to make use of the "pleasure principle" and so become an object of self-love[9].

However, it is only when the urges to procreate and to survive are recognized as being totally distinct, that certain common phenomena in human behavior become explicable.

For example, according to the Freudian understanding of human motivation, it should be a natural human drive to both have children and survive and prosper as individuals; taking action in one area should reinforce behavior in the other, as a logical outcome of the overall increase of the sex-drive's application in an individual's life. However, this is generally not the case. Most parents, when asked "How did having children affect your view of your own mortality?" will answer with some variation of "I became much more aware of my mortality, and reduced my risk-taking; if I die, who would take care of my child?". If this is followed up with the question "So who's life is more important to you, your own or your child's" the universal answer seems to be "my child's"[10]. The obvious conclusion that can be drawn from this is that the "survival" being striven for in the fulfillment of the sex-drive is not that of the parent's ego, but that of the parent's genes. The individual's survival, both ego and biological, becomes secondary to the survival of offspring.

If the wishes for individual survival and procreation were truly united in the sex-drive, neither the child's life nor the parent's would be more important to a parent. This is generally recognized to not be true; most parents are very conscious of the fact their offspring will outlive them, and not only accept this fact but make every effort to ensure their children are better off than they are themselves (although the Baby Boom generation may form an exception to this long-standing human trait). Parents often make sacrifices—sometimes extreme ones—to increase their children's prosperity or opportunities for such. It seems Freud may have been mistaken to have united the sex-drive and the will to live into a single class of instinct.

The will to live being referred to here is not only the motivating force for personal survival and advancement, but is also the driving force behind making unconscious behavior conscious. In other words, it is what makes both creativity and "personal growth" (i.e. the elimination or transmutation of dysfunctional behaviors) possible. Freud identifies the making of unconscious behavior conscious the very function and usefulness of psychology[11], so it seems a pity he so grossly devalues the human motivation that would seize on psychology as a tool to this end.

This belittling of the wish to survive, both by Freud in particular and the field of psychology in general, has helped reinforce the expression of the true Eros (Freud's name for the wish to procreate[12]) and that of the death-wish (named "Thanatos," the Greek god of death, by Paul Federn, one of the men that translated Freud's work into English) in individuals and in society. The increase of the homage paid to these two deities has come at the expense of the wish to survive, and create, and learn, which might explain why psychology has often been used first and best as a tool of manipulation, with its use as a tool for learning and healing coming in a distant second. After a century of Freud's teachings being examined and disseminated, they have served primarily to streamline the process of individuals repeating the unconscious behavior of those generations that came before them. Most of us still center our lives around finding a mate, procreating, securing some material goods for our offspring, and dying. This leaves little time and energy for things that might be more individually or collectively productive, such as questioning dysfunctional behavior or finding creative long-term solutions to problems.

While there is nothing wrong with procreation—it's how we all got here, after all—or in taking pleasure in the sex-act, the sex-drive's overarching priority in the majority of human lives (combined with the acting out of the death-wish being understood to be the only plausible alternative) prevents most people from becoming more conscious of themselves and the world around them. This helps explain many of the mistakes made by those of us who should know better, as well as why we continue to make these mistakes even after recognizing them.

In a generalized way, it can be said that the sex-drive belongs to the id, and the death-wish belongs to the super-ego. Both of these urges belong to and reinforce the influence of the subconscious mind in our lives. Even when consciously recognized, these urges continue to blindly drive the individual since the ego—the seat of consciousness—is not given the tools or encouragement it needs to counterbalance them effectively with the will to live.

The defining feature of the will to live is its empowerment of the ego. Since a "well-balanced" (i.e. healthy) individual requires full and constructive expression for the entire psyche, and since the ego has been sorely neglected, this may explain why psychology has failed to fulfill its potential for improving our individual and collective mental health. It may also explain why popular use of the term "ego"—usually used as a way of describing a person's self-importance—has strayed so far from Freud's original definition of the term (i.e. an individual's consciousness of him or herself as a distinct entity from the world around him or her).

It may be useful to look at one of the few examples in history of a group that has long separated the will to survive from the will to procreate, and which has given its members "sanctified" outlets for all three of the basic drives Freud identified: the Roman Catholic Church. Possibly the oldest and most powerful institution in continuous existence, there may be a connection between this institution's singular longevity, and the fact that it has long recognized and channeled the three fundamental drives under discussion like no other. Looking at the RCC through this lens, it seems clear that keeping the members of its controlling hierarchy—priests and the offices filled by priests, such as bishops, cardinals and the pope—celibate has concentrated libido in these controlling members' will to live. This will to live is then channeled toward the institution of the RCC, which has successfully created a resilient, devoted, and educable core for itself unmatched by any other group in history. Those who call themselves Catholic who are not part of the RCC hierarchy are often exhorted to "be fruitful and multiply" (i.e. have as many children as possible), which concentrates libido in the sex drive and the id. This behavior reduces creativity and induces docility in the masses of Catholic believers, causing them to behave very much like the "sheep" they are often referred to in Catholic doctrine. The "sheep" are told that the channeling of their libido towards procreation and away from the will to live is part of God's plan, provided of course that they fulfill certain conditions (e.g. attendance at Mass, tithing, seeking Church sanction for their marriage and for the education of their children) which happen to guarantee ever-flowing streams of income, influence, and new followers for the RCC. The death-wish of the organization's members is channeled into the concept of "damnation," and into the self-sacrifice required to avoid this terrible fate. As the ultimate degraded state of unlife and torment, damnation in Catholic doctrine is what awaits those living or dead who will not accept the RCC's authority. The avoidance of this state by Catholics, and the proselytizing to and persecution of non-believers by Catholics, not only acts as a further unification of the "faithful," but also gives Church members an outlet for those urges that arise out of the death-wish. This sanctification of guilt, self-sacrifice (including the more extreme forms of penance and martyrdom), witch-hunting, and even warfare in the name of the Church channels any aggressive drive—externalized death wish—its members may manifest away from the institution of the RCC and either direct it inward (causing these potential problem-member of the Church to self-destruct) or outward toward those the Church finds more generally "undesirable."

The specter of sexuality that has haunted the RCC almost from the beginning of its existence—from the difficulty many married people have staying "faithful" to one another, to the continued child-molestation exhibited by priests—has not significantly affected the RCC's moral authority or its ability to acquire and maintain great wealth and power. Other organizations that exhibit similar traits usually self-destruct in a very brief span of time. While it is possible that the RCC really does have the backing of an all-powerful divine being that maintains the institution's existence despite its human failings, it would appear that the explanation provided here of the RCC's unique channeling of the three basic human drives is at least as probable, and possibly more so, than continuous divine intervention.

Fulfillment of the wish to procreate, while reinforcing an individual's wish to survive in the short-term, reinforces the individual's wish to die in the long-term. This state of affairs has conspired to prevent most human endeavors from lasting more than a few generations, while it seems at least possible that an understanding and utilization of the full range of human instincts—the will to live, the sex-drive, and the death-wish—can build a thing nearly immune to the passage of time. To be properly understood, the wish to procreate cannot be seen as being united with the wish to live or the wish to die. The three wishes—to live, to procreate, and to die—must be acknowledged as the troika propelling human behavior that they are, if human motivations and energies are to be truly apprehended and effectively utilized. Once made conscious, knowledge of these motivations can aid an individual or group make more constructive choices in behavior and the allocation of resources.

Reinforcing unconscious human instinct, Freud told us that the psyche's genie only gives us two wishes to provide us purpose and meaning in life. Perhaps with this recognition that we have three wishes, not two, more of us will be able to bring forth the sanity and growth we have lacked before now.

Cause, Effect, Meaning

The term "meaning" is one that will be used throughout this section. The "meaning of meaning" has always been a very popular topic of discussion in philosophy[13], and especially in the post-modern age. When "all meaning is relative," it is very important to not only establish a functional definition of "meaning," but to stress the importance of using a common definition of the term if constructive discourse (i.e. discourse that increases understanding) is to be achieved.

So, then, what is the definition of "meaning" to be used here? According to the 4th Edition of the American Heritage Dictionary, once one gets past all the synonyms—"meaning" and "significance" are used to define each other—it seems that a thing's "meaning" is its level of importance to the perceiver. This two-dimensional understanding of the term, where something's "meaning" is determined by its importance relative to other things, does not cover its usage here in this text, and is brought up now so it can be discarded. For our purposes, "meaning" is much closer to the word "beauty," than it is to the word "importance". Something has "meaning" when it communicates an experience to the perceiver. As any discussion of a work of art, political event, or theological views between individuals will demonstrate, "meaning" is something different for each individual. Only concentrated effort toward reaching agreement by all parties involved in a discourse may provide a shared perception of meaning, and sometimes this shared perception is not possible even then. However, as is provable by any discourse between generations, or genders, or cultures, or individuals, establishing a shared perception of meaning—even if only partial—is essential if constructive discourse is to ensue. Therefore, the reader is asked to use the definition of "meaning" rendered above, that "meaning" is that which comes from a thing communicating an experience to a perceiver.

Immanuel Kant, in his "Critique of Pure Reason," stated that the recognition of cause-and-effect relationships is one of the defining characteristics of consciousness. Kant even went so far as to define "cause and effect" as one of his fundamental *categories* of thought[14], which as "pure concepts of the understanding," serve as the basis of all experience[15]. This recognition of the relationship between causality and consciousness has been a major contribution to our understanding of consciousness.

However, it seems Kant's elucidation may not have been complete in this area. While Kant discussed at great length cause-and-effect's role in defining consciousness, he did not appear to recognize that the ability to assign "meaning" (and so, one could argue, consciousness itself) to phenomena is necessary to define cause-and-effect. This lacuna in Kant's *a priori* description of consciousness may have prevented him—and all of us who have followed in his footsteps—from recognizing the "third dimension" of "meaning" that is intrinsic to the cause-and-effect relationship to consciousness.

For example, even though primitive humanity remained ignorant of the fact that one result of the sex-act was pregnancy, that ignorance never stopped babies from being born. Before the relationship between sex (as cause) and pregnancy (as effect) was perceived, humanity was no more able than any other animal to understand how and why pregnancy occurred in some females rather than in others, and at certain times rather than at other times. The cause-and-effect relationship between these things did not exist in the mind of primitive man (no matter how apparent it is to us now *a posteriori*), and so limited his consciousness. It was only when the consistent sequence of pregnancy following sex (and its opposite, the fact that pregnancy never happened without sex) was observed and then given the "meaning" of a cause-and-effect relationship, that a proper understanding of this phenomenon became possible. Adding the "third dimension" of "meaning" to cause-and-effect relationships allows us to better understand how and why discovery occurs in human experience.

The broadening of perception that comes with the understanding of "meaning's" intrinsic connection to "cause-and-effect" does not stop there, however. When we accept that not only do we, as conscious beings, *recognize* meaning when it is present in a phenomenon (at least under certain circumstances), but that we also can and do *assign* meaning to phenomena we encounter, there is another positive result: it allows for the understanding of how *causality*, *synchronicity*, and *coincidence* can occur in the same universe.

For our purposes here, *causality* is defined as the distinct action or effect which precipitates another distinct action or effect. *Synchronicity* is defined as a confluence of events mimicking a cause-and-effect relationship when no cause is apparently possible. *Coincidence* is defined as a confluence of events that have no apparent relation to each other at all, other than their relative proximity in space and time, if applicable.

To a mind that perceives the world in a strictly cause-and-effect way, all events must either have a cause, or be totally random. Human motivation, and free will, becomes a matter of choosing between pre-set alternatives. To a mind dominated by the cause-and-effect duality, if something has a cause there is only one valid meaning for that event, which limits the creation of meaning by individuals to effects caused by that person's actions. Other phenomena (the effects of others or non-sentient causes) can have their meaning apprehended, but that meaning will always originate outside the perceiver. A truly random event completely negates cause-and-effect, and so is rendered meaningless in a strictly cause-and-effect universe.

Since the perception of both *synchronicity* and *coincidence* seem inherent in human perception, as evidenced by the presence of mystics and atheists throughout the ages, scrutiny reveals that the cause-and-effect model is inadequate to produce complete understanding of the human perception of meaning. Even Kant's answer to the question of the human perception of meaning[16] (which has been considered definitive in all fields except perhaps that of religion for the last two hundred years or so) was defined by the idea of *causality*, and so remains unable to explain the co-existence of *synchronicity* and *coincidence* with *causality* in human perception.

Like other new understandings discussed in previous sections of this chapter, this one also requires clarification through the lens of an example. The ideas expressed in this book had a definite point of germination: it was in a bookstore, reading more-or-less simultaneously the Preface and Introduction of Jung's book "Psychological Types," and the first section of Campbell's book "Hero of a Thousand Faces" ("The Monomyth"). The reading of those pages of those two books, in conjunction with the other reading—and living—done up to that point by this author, was the *cause* whose *effect* was this book and the ideas expressed herein. Certain limitations of common understanding were suddenly perfectly clear, as a "new dimension" of the world seemed to unfold before this author's inner eye.

On the same night, upon leaving the bookstore where this epiphany occurred, a very busy intersection had to be crossed on foot. While the traffic light forbade pedestrian crossing in the required direction at that moment, no automobiles were actually present to impede the author's path across the street. In this way, events seemed to conspire in the author's favor for crossing the street. While these events mimicked a cause-and-effect relationship from the author's point of view—the author's desire to cross the street at that moment caused the effect of bringing him to the intersection at a time when traffic was absent—there was no way this author could have predicted when there would be a gap in the flow of traffic. The fortuitous absence of traffic at that moment, lacking a specific discernible cause, was an example of *synchronicity*, since it was a confluence of events given meaning by the author, as it helped facilitate his desire of the moment (crossing the street).

And finally, it was after sundown when all of this took place. The time of day had no apparent bearing on the events described in the previous two paragraphs, and so is a fine example of *coincidence*.

All of these events are perfectly understandable (i.e. definite, discrete, and usable meanings can be assigned to them) when the cause-effect-meaning model is applied to them, as already described. This is in contrast to how they appear when viewed through the dualistic lens of cause-and-effect. While the cause-and-effect model is superb at describing the meaning of the epiphany in the bookstore, it cannot accurately account for the experience of the *synchronicity* or the *coincidence* described above, without trying to turn them into things that they are not. In the two-dimensional cause-and-effect model of experience, cause must:

a.) Be absent in both the synchronicity and coincidence, rendering them both meaningless (although the ability to cross the intersection against the light certainly had meaning for the author, without requiring a definable cause), or

b.) Be present in the *synchronicity* (thereby redefining it as a cause-and-effect relationship) and absent in the *coincidence*, or

c.) Claim that all events have a "first cause" of some kind (i.e. Divine Will, the Big Bang, etc.) thereby rendering any other perception *or* assignment of meaning subordinate to this first cause, and so ultimately pointless.

Although all three of the ideas above have been presented at various times and in various ways as supposedly "deeper truths," none of the three intellectual contortions just listed offer a satisfactory explanation of how human beings experience events, because they all deny that human beings both subjectively assign and objectively perceive meaning in events. If individual human beings are incapable of perceiving and assigning meaning—or, if *causality* really is the only way to assign valid meaning to our experiences—then consciousness as we experience it shouldn't be possible. If only seeing things "the right way" (i.e. as cause and effect) produces consciousness, the experience of *synchronicity* and *coincidence* shouldn't exist.

This is not to say that an individual cannot be mistaken in the assignment or perception of meaning to phenomena. Obviously, such mistakes are quite common. It is only being argued here that the ability to assign and perceive meaning must be factored into our model of understanding, if this model is to accurately describe the co-existence of *causality*, *synchronicity* and *coincidence* in our experience.

One last point: since post-modernism postulates all structures as equivalent, and since any definition of meaning—a "meaning of meaning"—is a structure of language, and therefore (according to pomo) any definition of meaning is equivalent to any other, pomo claims that it is pointless to expend the effort to find a common perception of meaning. Since no shared perception of meaning is established, anyone involved in post-modern discourse (whether advocates of pomo or not) will almost certainly speak different languages—the words and arguments of any participant will be meaningless (or have different meaning) to every other, even if "English" or "French" or any other "language" is used in common by all participants in the given discourse—which makes communication awkward, and the possibility of constructive discourse (i.e. discourse that increases understanding) commensurately unlikely.

Odds and Ends

At this point, a restatement of some caveats mentioned earlier is in order. When seeking out phenomena or aspects of phenomena that are not dualistic, it is important to make sure that any additional axes of meaning revealed are not merely a different degree of an already apparent duality. As pointed out in Chapter 3, when identifying an additional axis of meaning to a black-and-white color scheme, a shade of grey is NOT a valid alternative, although it may at first appear so. A perception of a different color entirely—yellow, blue, red, etc.—rather than a variation or combination of black or white, is necessary if "color" is to be added or understood in one's vision. Keeping this in mind, the comprehension of non-dualistic phenomena is a fascinating and productive intellectual adventure. I wish the reader well in his or her explorations.

It is also important to note, once again, that in the kind of truly multi-polar world we appear to inhabit, a fixation on a specific kind of multi-polarity (e.g. tri-polarity) can be just as limiting as a fixation on duality. Keeping an open mind regarding the number of axes of experience any particular phenomenon may exhibit is vital if complete understanding is to be achieved.

As stated earlier, it is not the purpose of this work to "disprove" duality, since duality undeniably exists. However, this work does make the point that not everything can be understood as a duality.

Not only is there a way out of the dead-end much of 21st Century thought has reached, but new experiences and greater freedoms are available to us. It is merely necessary to think, experience, and create in new ways. These needed new freedoms and experiences will not come to us through re-analyzing our history to see where we went wrong, or resurrecting something already created and merely forgotten, or even by haphazardly tearing down what we have already built in the belief that the remains will find new life. It is a matter of claiming our birthright as conscious beings and creators, and each of us individually putting lie to the claim that "there is nothing new under the sun."

This book is meant to be a spring-board for the creativity and curiosity of its readers, not a definitive work that puts an end to all discourse. One could profitably view this book as a first pioneer's ship, that has sailed and now returns from unknown lands, bearing partial maps and a few useful treasures. It is up to further pioneers (and eventually the settlers) now departing to further explore—and finally inhabit—this new territory, and to discover the fullness of what it holds.

Conclusion

Kant, in his inimitable "Critique of Pure Reason," had this to say of those who "establish a science," or discover new ways of understanding:

"No one attempts to establish a science unless he has an idea on which to base it. But in the working out of the science the schema, nay even the definition which, at the start, he first gave the science, is very seldom adequate to his idea. For this idea lies hidden in reason, like a germ in which all the parts are still undeveloped and barely recognizable even under microscopic observation. Consequently, since sciences are devised from the point of view of a universal interest, we must not explain and determine them according to the description which their founder gives them, but in the conformity of the idea which, out of the natural unity of the parts that we have assembled, we find to be grounded in reason itself. For we shall then find that its founder, and often even his latest successors, are groping for an idea which they have never succeeded in making clear to themselves, and that consequently they have not been in a position to determine the proper content, the articulation (systematic unity), and limits of the science."[1]

The tool for producing understanding created—germinated—by Descartes, and nurtured by Kant, had not yet reached its full maturation in Kant's treatment. Sadly, the attentions given this science by Hegel, Nietzsche, and especially the post-modernists have on balance not produced a growth, but a stunting of Descartes' and Kant's carefully tended process of understanding, both in principle and in application. This mutilation of understanding is a problem which threatens our very ability to reason, and cannot be dealt with simply by going back to where we went wrong, writing off everything since and hoping for the best. Such an approach makes the repetition of the same mistakes likely, if not certain.

What is false or incomplete in our understanding must not only be recognized as such, but new possibilities for growth beyond these shortcomings must be identified and proven to work. The incomplete must be made complete, and the false contrasted with what is true. That is what this book has attempted to do, to suggest and demonstrate a useable way out of the impasses and destructive behavior modern understanding has led us in to. As Kant advises us, we must verify our *a priori* models with repeated empirical proof. We have returned to Kant, and after recognizing the bad—and the good—of the path tread by him and his successors, we have begun our expansion of understanding beyond Kant.

Descartes and Kant were both attempting to "establish a science," Descartes to find a system which would make all of existence comprehensible, Kant to make what he called metaphysics (i.e. the study of god, freedom and immortality[2]) into a respectable "science". Both men were true to the form of Kant's description of such pioneers: their understandings and definitions were incomplete and contained many inaccuracies, but made greater and more accurate understandings and definitions possible to those who came after them. This book, while discussing the limits of these two men's thoughts and showing a way beyond them, is also an expression of the growth of the principles laid down by these two men. This treatise is not a wholesale rejection of Descartes' and Kant's ideas and process of understanding (or even of those others who came after them), but a recognition of both the limitations and uses of their ideas and the process that brought them about, transcending the mere analysis of their conclusions.

Also described in these pages is a different process of understanding, which seems to clarify some of the issues the C-K-H process has left opaque. This provides us with an expansion of human knowledge and consciousness, surpassing that provided by Descartes and Kant, while furthering their original goal: The improvement of humanity, through expanded consciousness.

Of course, the analysis of non-dualistic phenomena presented here may prove to be a new science in and of itself. It would be wonderful, if that does prove to be true. As the quote from Kant that began this Conclusion would imply, this would mean that there is so much more you, the reader, have the opportunity to discover.

Notes

Introduction

What Happened

1. "Principles," Descartes Chap. 1 Principle VII
2. see also Veitch/Sorell pp135-6
3. Veitch/Sorell Intro pp xv-xviii
4. Veitch/Sorell Intro p xxviii
5. Veitch/Sorell Intro p xxviii
6. Strictly speaking, it should be understood that it is the "main theories" of modern western philosophy, such as analytic philosophy, pragmatism, existentialism, structuralism, and post-structuralism, whose descent can be directly traced to Kant's Critique of Pure Reason. While moral philosophy, political philosophy, and the philosophy of science technically lay outside the Critique's direct line of descent, they (like most other fields of study in the 19th, 20th, and 21st Centuries) still cannot be said to be outside its influence.
7. Critique of Pure Reason, Immanuel Kant Intro Sect. I
8. Ibid. Intro Section II paragraphs 1-2
9. Ibid. Intro Section III
10. Ibid. Intro Sect. IV
11. Ibid. Intro Sect. IV-V
12. Ibid. pp 100, 297
13. Ibid. pp 100, 297
14. Ibid. pp98-9
15. Ibid. pp xvi-xxi
16. Ibid. Book One Second Division
17. Ibid. pp13-4, 21
18. Ibid. pp98, 100
19. Ibid. Intro Sect V
20. Science of Logic, Hegel, pp178-84, 190-8, 204-11, 223, 234-37
21. Ibid. pp82-6

22. Ibid. Chapters of same names
23. Ibid. pp212-7, 227-34, 238-313
24. Thus Spake Zarathustra, Friedrich Nietzsche, #1
25. Ibid. Prologue #2, and most of the rest of the book
26. Ibid. #1
27. "Human, All Too Human," Nietzsche, #1
28. see Kant's "Critique of Pure Reason" and Hegel's "Science of Logic"

What's Happening

1. "The Origin of Species," Charles Darwin, Chap IV
2. Kant, pp545-6
3. "Relativity: The Special and General Theory," Albert Einstein, p15
4. Ibid. p71
5. Ibid. p72
6. Ibid. p55
7. Ibid. p56
8. Ibid. p70
9. see "Critique of Pure Reason" footnote quoted in Chap. 1
10. "The Elegant Universe," Brian Greene, pp94-105
11. Ibid. pp112-3
12. Ibid. pp108-11
13. Ibid. p111
14. Ibid. p110
15. Ibid. pp117-31, see footnote 8 on Greene p131
16. "The Ego and the Id," Sigmund Freud, pp3-4
17. Ibid. p5
18. Ibid. pp8-9
19. Ibid. p10
20. Ibid. p19
21. Ibid. pp18-9
22. Ibid. pp22-3, 26, 30-6

23. Ibid. pp26-30
24. Ibid. pp37-8
25. Ibid. pp38-9
26. Ibid. pp42-5
27. Ibid. pp44-5
28. Ibid. pp19, 45
29. Ibid. p48
30. Ibid. pp37, 47, 57-9
31. Ibid. pp31-2
32. Ibid. p56
33. Ibid. p49
34. Ibid. pp56-7, 59-62
35. Ibid. pp57-9
36. Ibid. pp3-7, footnotes
37. "The General Theory of Employment, Interest, and Money," J. M. Keynes, pp17-8, 32
38. Ibid. p33
39. Ibid. p25
40. Ibid. Chap. 3
41. Ibid. Chap. 2 Sec. VI, last paragraph
42. Ibid. Chap 7 Sec. II
43. Ibid. Chap 7 Sec. II
44. Kant pp98-9
45. "Capitalism and Freedom," Milton Friedman, Chaps. III, IV, V, VI, VII, and XI
46. Ibid. Chap III
47. Ibid. pp14-5
48. Ibid. p15
49. Ibid. pp69-70
50. Ibid. pp29-30
51. "Writing and Difference," Jacques Derrida, p28
52. TSZ Intro Sec. 4

53. "Introduction to Metaphysics," Martin Heidegger p83, "The Order of Things," Michel Foucault, pp385-6, Derrida pp4, 28-30
54. Heidegger pp83-4
55. Foucault pp299-300
56. Foucault p386
57. Heidegger p10
58. Derrida pp29-30
59. Heidegger pp63-4, 126-33
60. Foucault pp312-8
61. Foucault pp315-6
62. see discussion of Hegel's proof of Science of Logic's superiority to mathematics in Chap. 1 of this book, and footnote 22 in Chap. 1
63. TSZ #5

A Brief Analysis
1. Keynes Chap 7 Sec II

What Could Happen
1. Modern Age Vol. 45 no. 3, "Ways Out of the Post-Modern Discourse"
2. Hegel pp333-74
3. Smith p31
4. Freud Chap. IV
5. Freud pp37, 38
6. Freud p38
7. Freud pp54-6
8. Freud p55
9. Freud pp24-5
10. research conducted by the author
11. Freud p5

12. Freud p37
13. "Modern Age: A Quarterly Review," Vol. 45, number 3, Summer 2003, Intercollegiate Studies Institute, p197
14. Kant pp113, 185 and elsewhere
15. Kant pp147, 160-1, 170-1
16. Kant pp464-79

Conclusion
1. Kant pp654-5
2. Kant p46

Bibliography

"A Discourse on Method, Meditations, and Principles," Rene Descartes, translated by John Veitch, edited by Tom Sorell, first included in Everyman Library in 1912, Orion Publishing Group/Tuttle Publishing

"Critique of Pure Reason," [unabridged edition] Immanuel Kant, translated by Norman Kemp Smith, copyright Macmillan & Co. Ltd. 1929, Bedford/St. Martin's

"Science of Logic," Georg Wilhelm Friedrich Hegel, translated by A.V. Miller, copyright George Allen and Unwin Ltd., Humanity Books

"Thus Spake Zarathustra," Friedrich Nietzsche, translated by Thomas Common, Prometheus Books

"Human, All Too Human," Friedrich Nietzsche, translated by Marion Faber, copyright 1984 University of Nebraska Press

"The Origin of Species," Charles Darwin, Mentor Books copyright 1958

"Relativity: The Special and General Theory," Albert Einstein, translated by Robert W. Lawson, copyright 2001 Dover Publications Inc.

"The Elegant Universe," Brian Greene, copyright 1999 Brian Green, Vintage Books

"The Ego and the Id," Sigmund Freud, translated by Joan Riviere, copyright 1960 James Strachey, W.W. Norton & Co.
"The General Theory of Employment, Interest, and Money," John Maynard Keynes, copyright 1964 First Harvest/Harcourt

"Capitalism and Freedom," Milton Friedman, copyright 1962, 1982, 2002 The University of Chicago, The University of Chicago Press

"An Introduction To Metaphysics," Martin Heidegger, translated by Ralph Manheim, copyright 1959 Yale University Press, Yale University PressInc.

"The Order of Things," Michel Foucault, copyright 1970 Random House Inc., Vintage Books edition April 1994

"Writing and Difference," Jacques Derrida, translated by Alan Bass, copyright 1978 The University of Chicago Press

"Modern Age: A Quarterly Review," Vol. 45, number 3, Summer 2003, Intercollegiate Studies Institute
  "Ways Out of the Postmodern Discourse," Ewa M. Thompson

"American Heritage Dictionary," copyright 2000 Houghton Mifflin Company

"An Inquiry Into The Nature and Causes of the Wealth of Nations," [complete and unabridged] Adam Smith, 2000 Modern Library Paperback Edition

"The Basic Writings of Sigmund Freud," translated/edited by A.A. Brill, copyright 1995 Random House Inc., 1995 Modern Library edition

www.ingramcontent.com/pod-product-compliance
Lightning Source LLC
Chambersburg PA
CBHW072203090426
42740CB00012B/2363